Simply SAMPLERS

Simply SAMPLERS

Easy Techniques for Hand Embroidery

A NeedleKnowledge® Book

Cheryl Fall

STACKPOLE
BOOKS

Published by
STACKPOLE BOOKS
5067 Ritter Road
Mechanicsburg, PA 17055
www.stackpolebooks.com

Note: Every effort has been made to ensure the accuracy and completeness of the material presented in this book. Neither the publisher nor the author assumes responsibility for errors, typographical mistakes, variations in an individual's work, or the use of materials other than those specified.

Printed in the United States of America

10 9 8 7 6 5 4 3 2 1

FIRST EDITION

Cover design by Caroline Stover

Library of Congress Cataloging-in-Publication Data

Fall, Cheryl, author.
Simply samplers : easy techniques for hand embroidery / Cheryl Fall. — First edition.
pages cm — (A needleknowledge book)
ISBN 978-0-8117-1292-7
1. Embroidery. I. Title.
TT770.F355 2014
746.44—dc23

2014014847

This book is dedicated to my stitching friends.
They are a continuing source of encouragement, inspiration,
needlework fellowship, and a good laugh now and then.

Contents

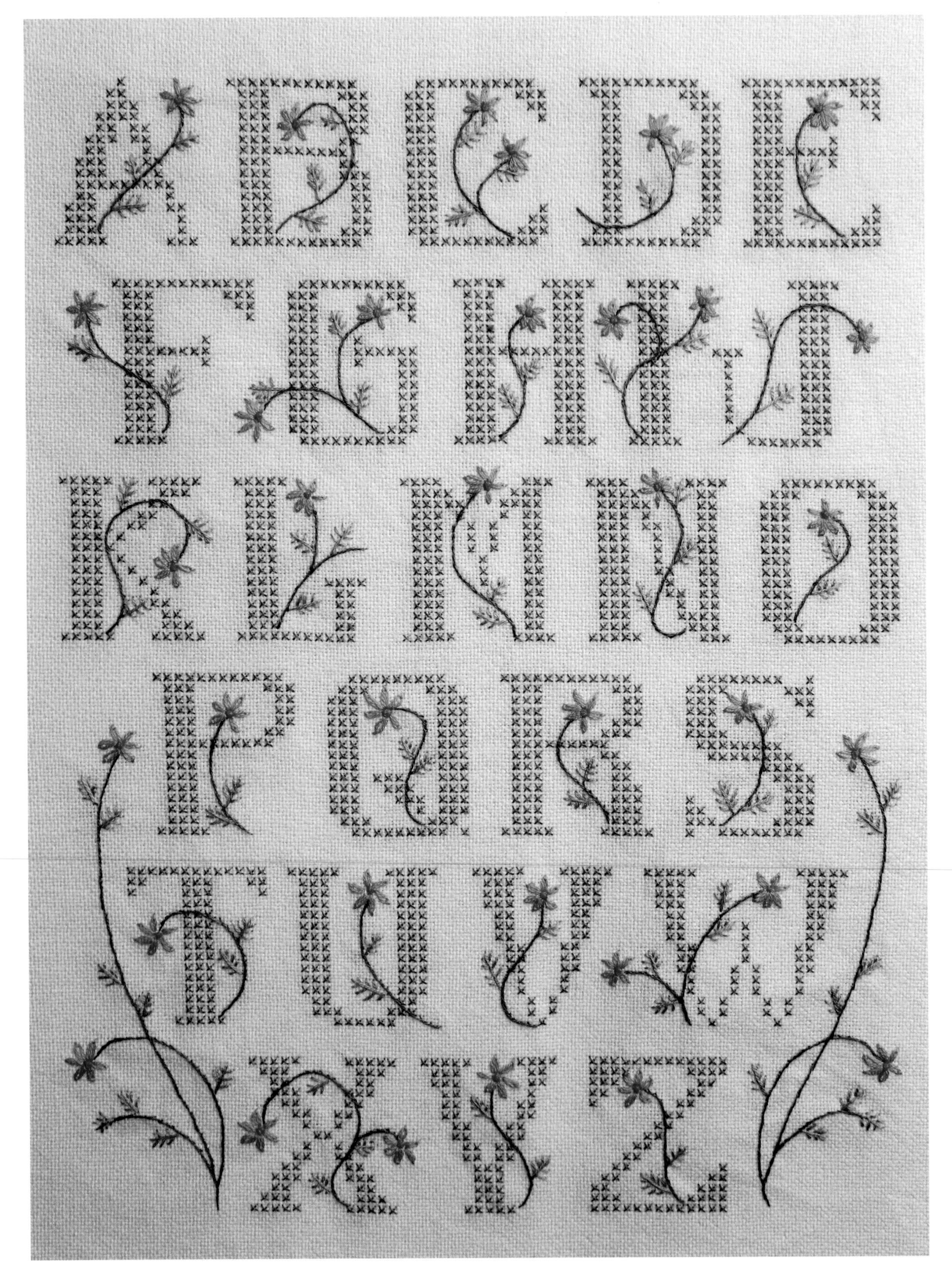

Preface

What is a sampler? When most people think of samplers, they think of cross-stitch projects featuring an alphabet and traditional motifs. But a sampler is so much more! In a nutshell, a sampler is a "sampling" of different stitches or different motifs stitched on fabric to form a pattern or learn a particular technique.

At one time samplers were used as a learning tool to teach young girls the needlework skills necessary for daily living, including darning, mending, and general sewing, as well as ways to add decorative embroidered elements to basic household items. The most common decorative embroidery techniques taught while working a sampler included cross-stitch, counted-thread stitches, darning stitch, and surface embroidery stitches.

In this book you will learn to work an assortment of sampler types, from colorful modern band samplers to traditional alphabet samplers, in a variety of techniques. You'll build your stitch repertoire with each new technique you learn, much as young girls did in the past.

This book contains 24 different sampler designs that you can stitch, including smaller projects inspired by their larger and more involved counterparts. Full-size patterns are provided for the surface samplers, and detailed charts or diagrams are included for the counted-thread projects. Diagrams for all of the stitches used in the projects are provided as well, starting on page 73, and you can finish your projects using the basic finishing instructions in the final chapter.

So pack your workbag, select your project, and grab your floss . . . it's time to stitch!

Supplies and Tools

Fabrics

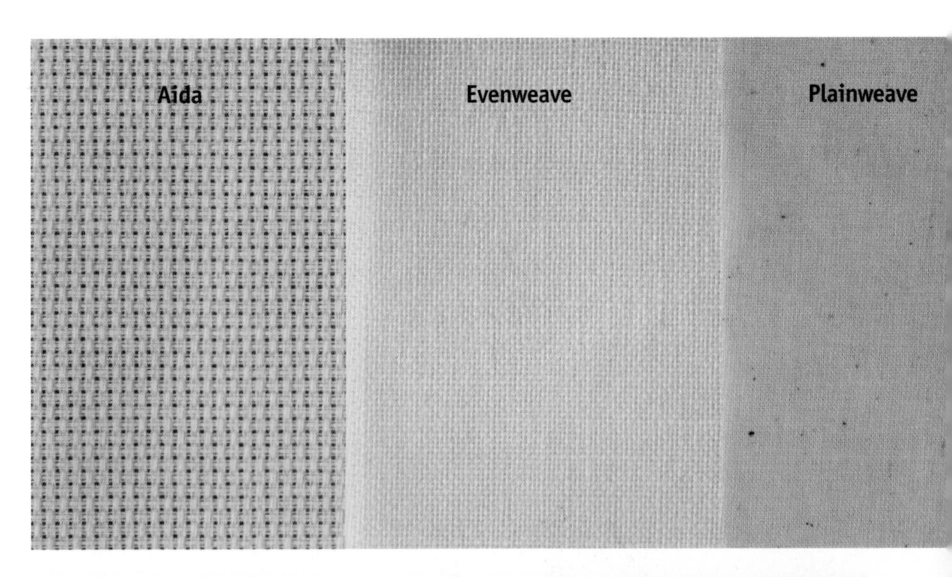

The projects in this book are made using fabrics that you can find readily at your local needlework shop, hobby and craft chain, or sewing store, or through online sources. The types of fabric you will use are Aida, evenweave, and plainweave.

Aida is a fabric that is specially woven for cross-stitch, with a weave that contains an even number of vertical and horizontal squares per inch. It is available in a wide variety of counts—the number of squares—per inch. The fabrics used in this book range from 11 to 16 count. Refer to the project instructions for the count used in each sampler.

Evenweave fabrics have an even number of vertical and horizontal (warp and weft) threads per inch in a plain weave. They are used for the counted-thread projects in this book, as well as some of the cross-stitch samplers. When working cross-stitch on evenweave, the pattern will state the number of threads to cross when working the stitches.

Plainweave fabrics are tightly woven evenweave fabrics with threads that are too close together to count. These firmer fabrics are used for the surface-embroidered samplers in this book.

All fabrics should be edge-finished with machine zigzag stitching around the edges to prevent fraying while you're working the stitching.

Threads

Cotton 6-strand embroidery floss is used for all of the projects in this book. This floss is made from six individual strands of thread that can be divided into smaller groups of thread. In most cases, two strands are used for cross-stitch and surface embroidery and a single strand for backstitch or accent stitching.

Specialty threads have been used in some of the projects to add metallic sparkle or a multicolored look, and these flosses are also divisible. Refer to the project instructions for the number of threads to be used while working a project.

When shopping for threads online, especially if you are planning on making color substitutions, remember that although the label may indicate the thread is colorfast, it may in fact smudge or bleed when laundered. Unfortunately, new and revised FDA rules in the U.S., and similar rules abroad, have caused changes in dye formulations, making few dyes truly colorfast. While this is meant to keep stitchers safe from harmful chemicals, it can also cause color variations if mixing an old skein of a certain color with a newer skein.

TIP: Make sure you have enough of each thread color to complete a project. The older the thread, the greater the chance that the exact color is no longer available.

Manufacturers should not be blamed for this. They go through great pains to ensure the accuracy of their colors and must conform to the rules regarding chemicals in dyes to stay in business and continue providing you with quality needlework threads. However, despite their best efforts, the changes in formulation often do cause a difference in color. To avoid this, be sure to compare the actual color of new and old threads before stitching.

Needles

Just three types of needles are called for when working the samplers: tapestry, embroidery, and beading needles.

Tapestry needles have a blunt tip and a long eye that can accommodate several strands of embroidery floss. The blunt tips allow the needle to pass between the warp and weft fibers in the fabric without catching them, which helps make well-formed stitches.

Embroidery needles have sharp tips and eyes that can accommodate several strands of floss. The sharp tips allow the needle to pierce the fibers in the fabric, rather than passing next to them. These needles are used for the surface-embroidery samplers, or where surface embroidery has been used to add accents to counted-thread and cross-stitch designs.

Beading needles have long, thin shafts and a small eye that can only accommodate a single strand of thread. These needles are used to attach beads or embellishments to a project.

Refer to the directions for needle sizes, or use the table below to select the right needle for your project.

TIP: Blunt tapestry needles pass through the space between two threads in an evenweave fabric or between the squares in Aida fabric, while sharp embroidery needles pierce the fibers in plainweave embroidery fabrics.

Fabric Count	Needle Size	Needle Type
6-count Aida	Size 18	Tapestry (blunt)
8-count Aida	Size 20	Tapestry (blunt)
11-count Aida	Size 22	Tapestry (blunt)
14-count Aida	Size 24	Tapestry (blunt)
16-count Aida	Size 26	Tapestry (blunt)
18-count Aida	Size 28	Tapestry (blunt)

Strand Count	Needle Size	Needle Type
1–2-strand floss	Size 10	Embroidery (sharp)
3–4-strand floss	Size 9 or 8	Embroidery (sharp)
5–6-strand floss	Size 8	Embroidery (sharp)
Size 5 Pearl Cotton	Size 6	Embroidery (sharp)
Size 8 Pearl Cotton	Size 8	Embroidery (sharp)
Size 12 Pearl Cotton	Size 10	Embroidery (sharp)

Scissors, Hoops, and Notions

In addition to the needles, threads, and fabrics, there are other items you will need to work the projects in this book. These are notions that are a basic part of any embroidery or sewing workbag and include scissors in several sizes (large shears for cutting fabric and small embroidery scissors for cutting thread), embroidery hoops in several sizes and shapes to hold the fabric taut while working the stitching, a measuring tape or ruler, and pens or pencils for marking the cloth or transferring a design to your fabric.

TIP: Completely separate all strands of embroidery floss and regroup them before using them. This will result in a smoother finished stitch and helps prevent tangling.

Other handy items to keep in your bag include thimbles, tweezers, a nail file in case of burrs, thread conditioner for use with unruly threads, a magnetic needle keeper, plastic or cardboard bobbins for wrapping leftover embroidery threads for safekeeping, and a stitch guide.

Basic Techniques

Starting and Ending Your Thread

The first rule of embroidery is: No knots—not ever—unless they are an integral part of the design. Knots are not only unnecessary, but they can come undone after the project is used or laundered, causing stitch loss, which results in bumps and ugly tails on the back side of the work. Instead of using a knot, your thread should always start and end with a tail of thread that passes underneath the thread on the back side of the work. There are two easy ways to do this at the beginning of your work.

A *waste knot* can be made when working cross-stitch or counted-thread projects. To use a waste knot, place your knot so that it will be directly in the line of stitching. Once you have overstitched the tail of the thread, clip the knot and trim the tail.

An *away knot* is a temporary knot that is made a few inches from where your stitching is set to begin and is handy for surface embroidery projects. After you have completed stitching the area, the knot is clipped from the piece, the resulting tail threaded through the eye of the needle, and the tail woven through the stitching on the back side of the work.

With both techniques, the thread should be woven through the stitching on the back side of the work when ending off.

Keeping your work knot-free with these techniques is easy peasy, so no excuses.

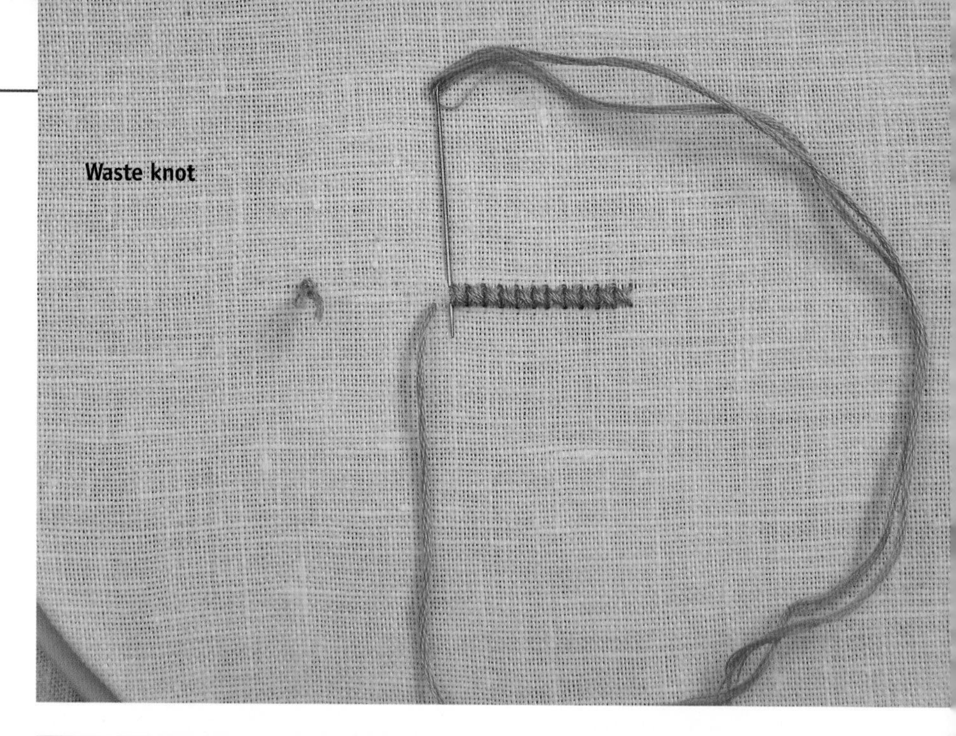
Waste knot

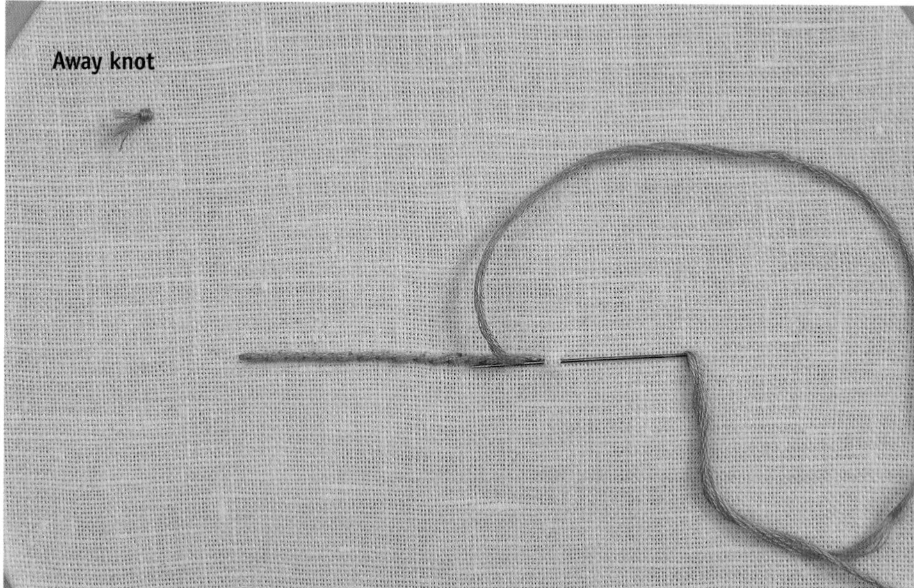
Away knot

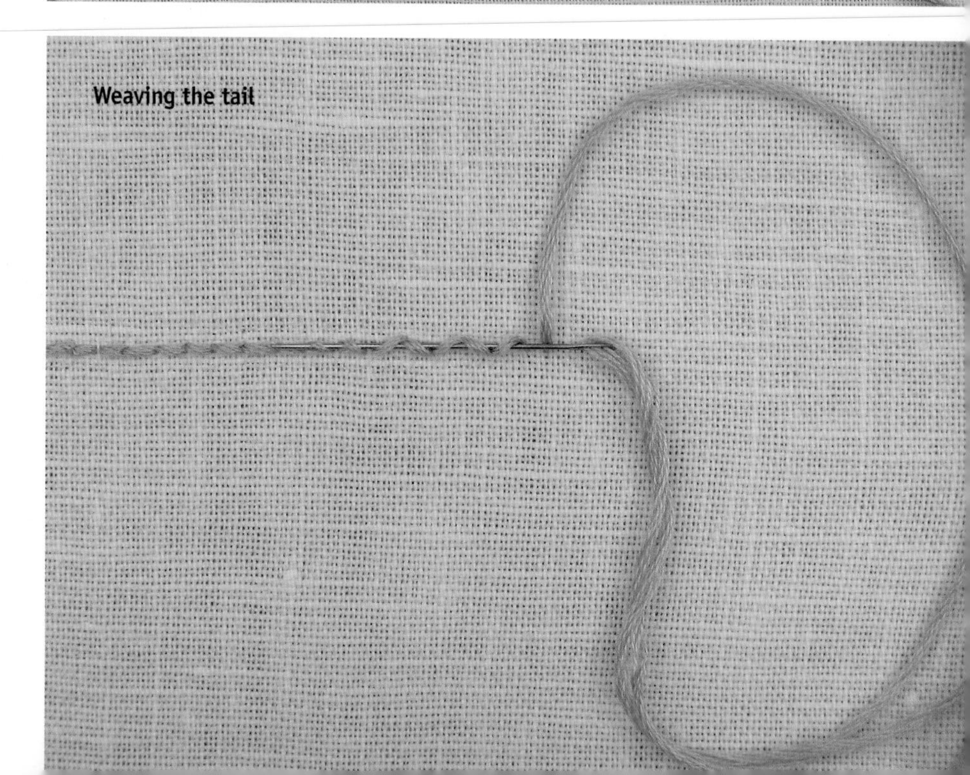
Weaving the tail

Determining and Changing Thread Count

All of the designs in this book tell you what fabric was used to make the sample shown in the photograph. However, if you wish to use a piece of fabric that you already have in your stash, but are unsure what the finished size of the piece will be, here's the simple math:

1. Determine the number of stitches along the top (horizontal) edge and one side (vertical) edge of the pattern. This can be done by counting the number of squares in the pattern grid. To make things easier, there are 10 small squares for each larger square in the grid.
2. Divide the numbers from step 1 by the thread count. In this example I am using a pattern that is 60 vertical stitches by 80 horizontal stitches:
   - 6-count Aida yields a finished size of 10" x 13.33"
   - 8-count Aida yields a finished size of 7.5" x 10"
   - 11-count Aida yields a finished size of 5.45" x 7.27"
   - 14-count Aida yields a finished size of 4.28" x 5.71"
   - 16-count Aida yields a finished size of 3.75" x 5"

Find the Centers

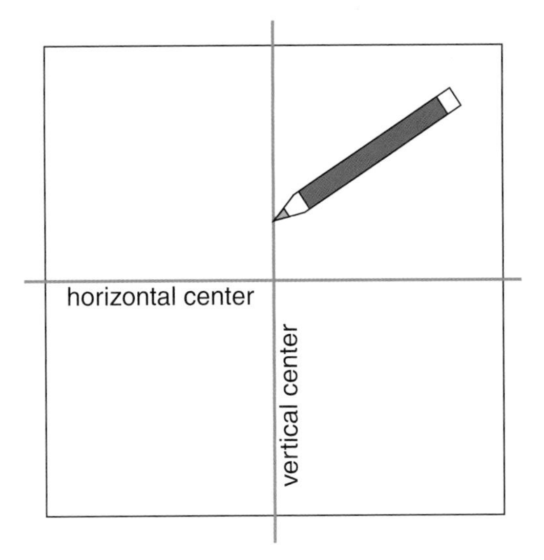

Fold the fabric into quarters and mark the vertical and horizontal centers. Using a washable, water-soluble marking pen or pencil (not a permanent pen or heat transfer pen), draw a line along a single fiber of fabric to mark the centers. Or, using a single strand of 6-strand floss, mark the centers using running stitch along the ditch between two strands of warp and weft threads in the fabric.

Transferring a Design to Fabric

Designs for surface embroidery can be transferred to the surface of the fabric using several different transfer methods.

The easiest method is to trace the design directly onto the fabric using a water-soluble fabric marking pen or pencil. To do this, place the pattern over a light source, such as a window or light box, and center the fabric over the pattern. You should be able to see the design through the fabric and trace it.

You can also use transfer paper made for fabric, which you can find at any sewing or fabric store, to mark the design on the fabric. Place the fabric on a hard surface and place a sheet of transfer paper ink-side-down on the fabric. (The transfer ink side of the paper often has a powdery or waxy feeling to it if you have difficulty determining which side the ink is on.) Center the pattern over the transfer paper and trace the design using a ballpoint pen or stylus.

Tracing designs to heavy fabrics can be done with a technique called *thread tracing*. To transfer using this method, trace the pattern onto a lightweight piece of tracing paper or pattern tissue. Thread a needle with a length of fine thread in a contrasting color. Stitching through both the paper and the fabric, work the running stitch or back stitch along all the marked lines in the pattern. Remove the paper and the thread lines remain on the fabric. Work the final stitching over these fine-stitched lines.

Reversed pattern traced on lightweight paper

Heat transfer pens and pencils or ready-made hot-iron transfer patterns can also be used for marking an embroidery pattern. Keep in mind that these markings are permanent and must be completely covered by the embroidery stitches or they will always show on the finished project.

When transferring a design to fabric using this method, remember that you will be creating a mirror image of the design. This means that the design needs to be traced onto the paper using the transfer pen or pencil in *reverse*. While this may not be much of a problem with repeating designs, it's critical for one-way designs and text.

Following the manufacturer's directions and using the proper pressing techniques when transferring a design with this method is essential. Your goal is to have a fine, smooth line to stitch along instead of a smeared line that is difficult to cover.

To press the design onto the fabric properly, never use a side-to-side motion when moving the iron from one area to another. This causes the ink to smear. Instead, carefully lift the iron, move it to the next location, and press downwards.

Remove paper pattern after heat transfer to fabric

Reading a Chart

It's easiest to follow a pattern by working from the center outwards. You can locate the center of the pattern by finding the arrows along the outside edge of the grid and noting where they intersect.

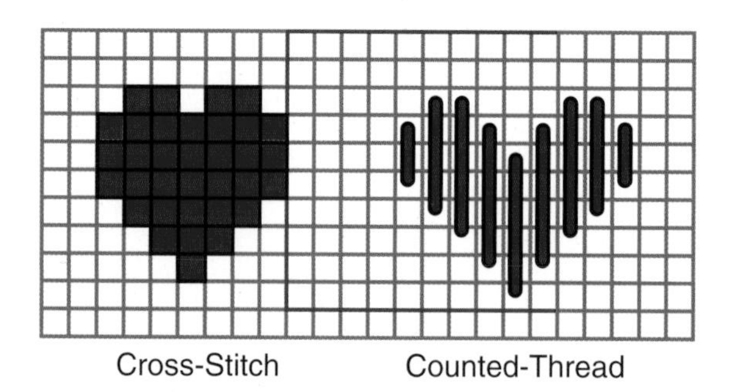

Cross-Stitch Counted-Thread

There are two types of charts used in this book: cross-stitch and counted. The charts used for cross-stitch feature small colored squares on a grid. One square in the grid is the equivalent of one stitch on the fabric.

Counted charts are also given on a grid; however, the grid represents the vertical and horizontal (warp and weft) threads in the fabric, rather than the individual stitches. On this type of chart, the stitch is shown passing between and over the threads in the fabric. Don't let this scare you. These charts are very easy to follow.

Adding Color to Embroidery

You can easily add color to embroidery with wax-based colored pencils, such as those made by PrismaColor. The color should be added after you have completed the stitching and have washed, dried, and pressed the piece. Coloring should not be done on pieces that will be used often or laundered.

When coloring, use a light touch and add color in a circular motion to avoid having pronounced warp and weft color lines in your fabric. Do not press to make the colors darker, because this will only highlight imperfections in the fabric or threads on the underside. Instead, build the color up in layers, shading naturally as you build the layers.

Once you have finished coloring the design, place a piece of unbleached muslin over the design and press the piece with a hot iron to set the wax-based pencils. This helps prevent loss of color from handling.

Embellishments for Samplers

Samplers can be embellished with beads, buttons, charms, and trims to add interest to a piece. These elements should be added after the stitching has been completed and any temporary markings have been removed from the fabric.

Sampler Projects

PROJECT 1

Spanish Lace Sampler with Matching Scissor Fob

SKILL LEVEL: **INTERMEDIATE**

Stitch a classical sampler set using cross-stitch and backstitch in a Spanish lace design using variegated red floss. The set includes a square sampler and a smaller square design that can be finished as a scissor fob, ornament, or pincushion. Select one of the letters from the alphabet to use in the center of the small square to customize it for yourself or a friend.

Just a single color of floss is used, so you can easily swap another color for the red. Variegated blue, black, or a multicolored over-dyed thread would work equally well.

Materials

- 18 x 18-inch piece of 28-count white or antique white evenweave linen for sampler
- 6 x 6-inch piece of 28-count white or antique white linen for the smaller design
- DMC 6-strand embroidery floss in color 115 Variegated Red
- Size 24 tapestry needle

Directions

1. Fold the fabric into quarters and mark the vertical and horizontal centers.
2. Work the cross-stitch areas over two threads of the evenweave fabric using 2 strands of the 6-strand floss. Work from the center outwards.
3. When working the lacy trim, use a single strand of floss and the Holbein stitch or backstitch.
4. Frame the sampler and finish the ornament, referring to the Finishing Touches chapter.

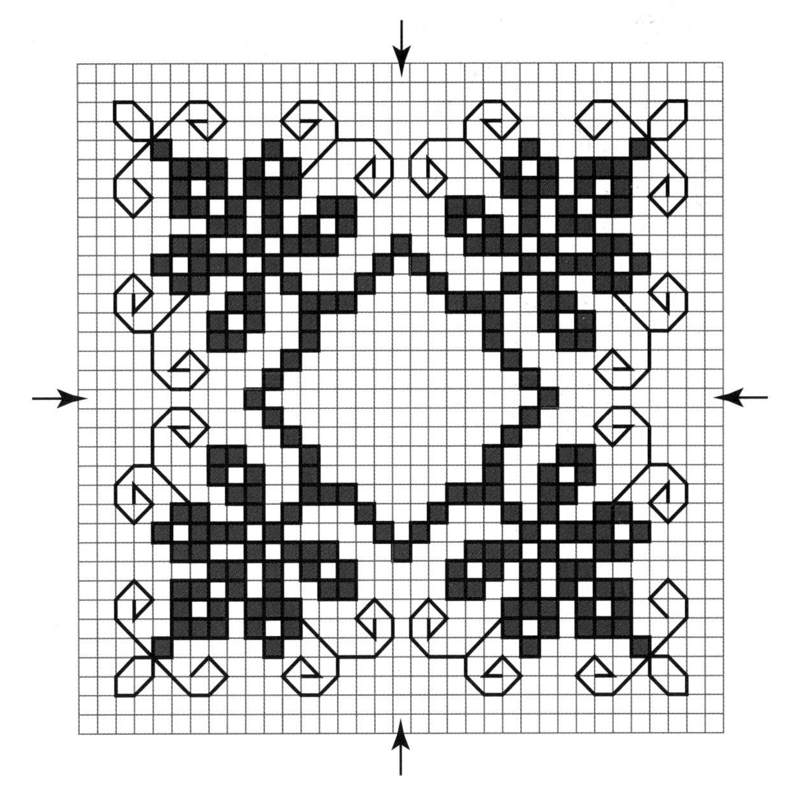

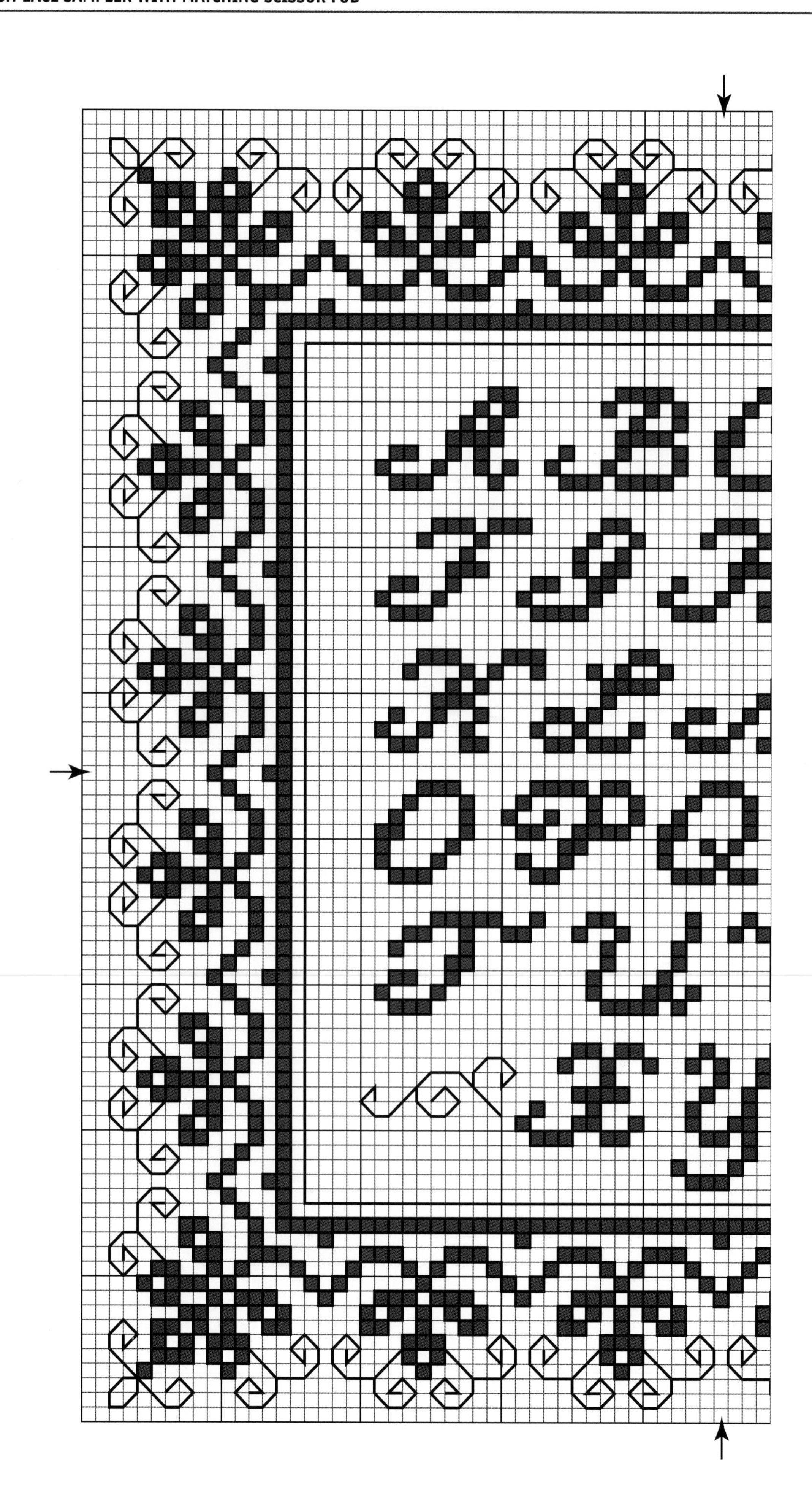

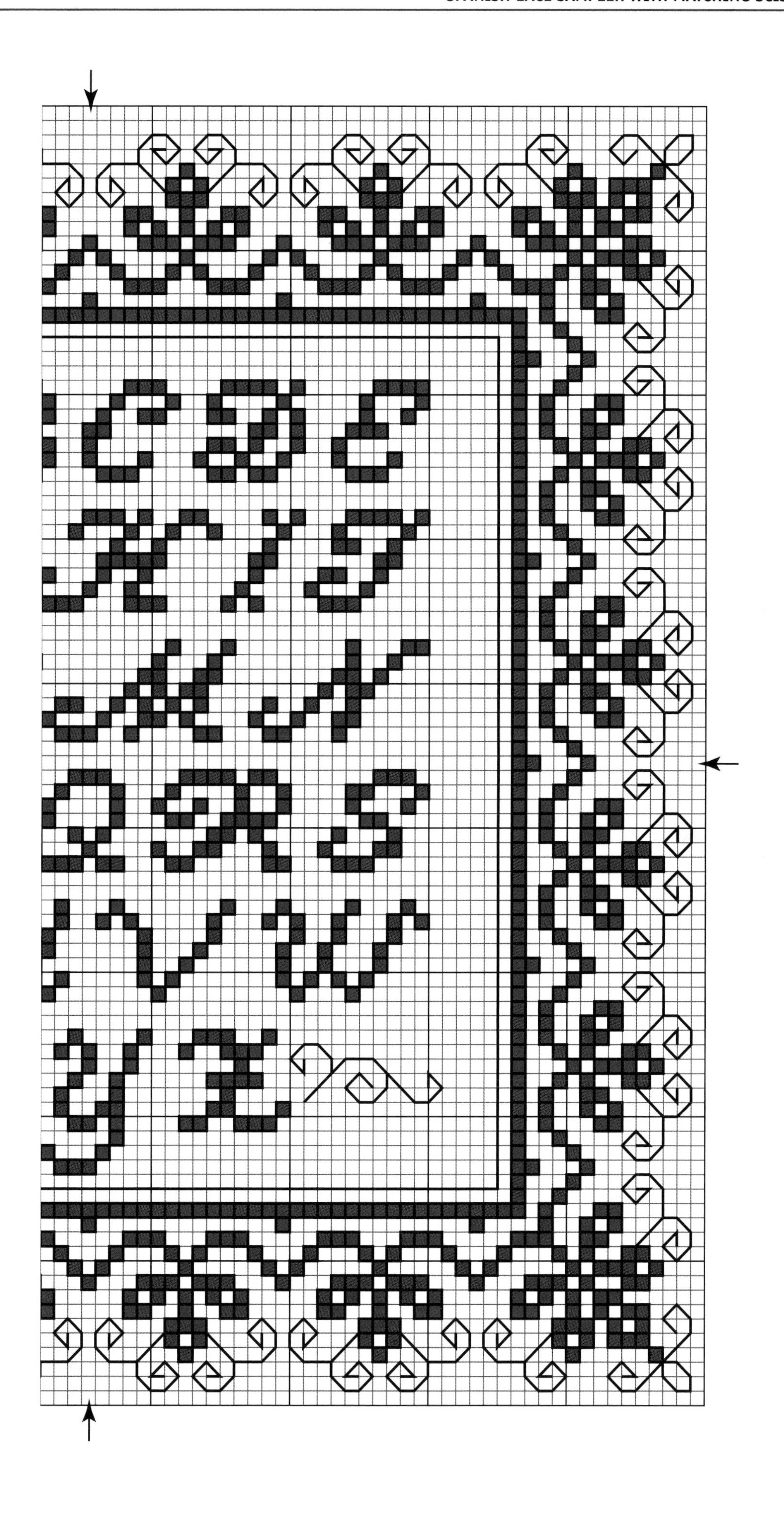

PROJECT 2

Mini Alphabet Sampler

SKILL LEVEL: **BEGINNER**

Stitch this fun little sampler in bright shades of blended or over-dyed embroidery floss for a pop of color. Finish the project as a mini accent pillow, an ornament, or a pincushion. I've also framed the piece, which is designed to fit a standard 4 x 5-inch picture frame.

Materials

- 8 x 10-inch piece of white 14-count Aida
- 1 skein of DMC Color Variations 6-strand floss in colors 4200 Wildfire or 4022 Mediterranean Sea
- Size 24 tapestry needle

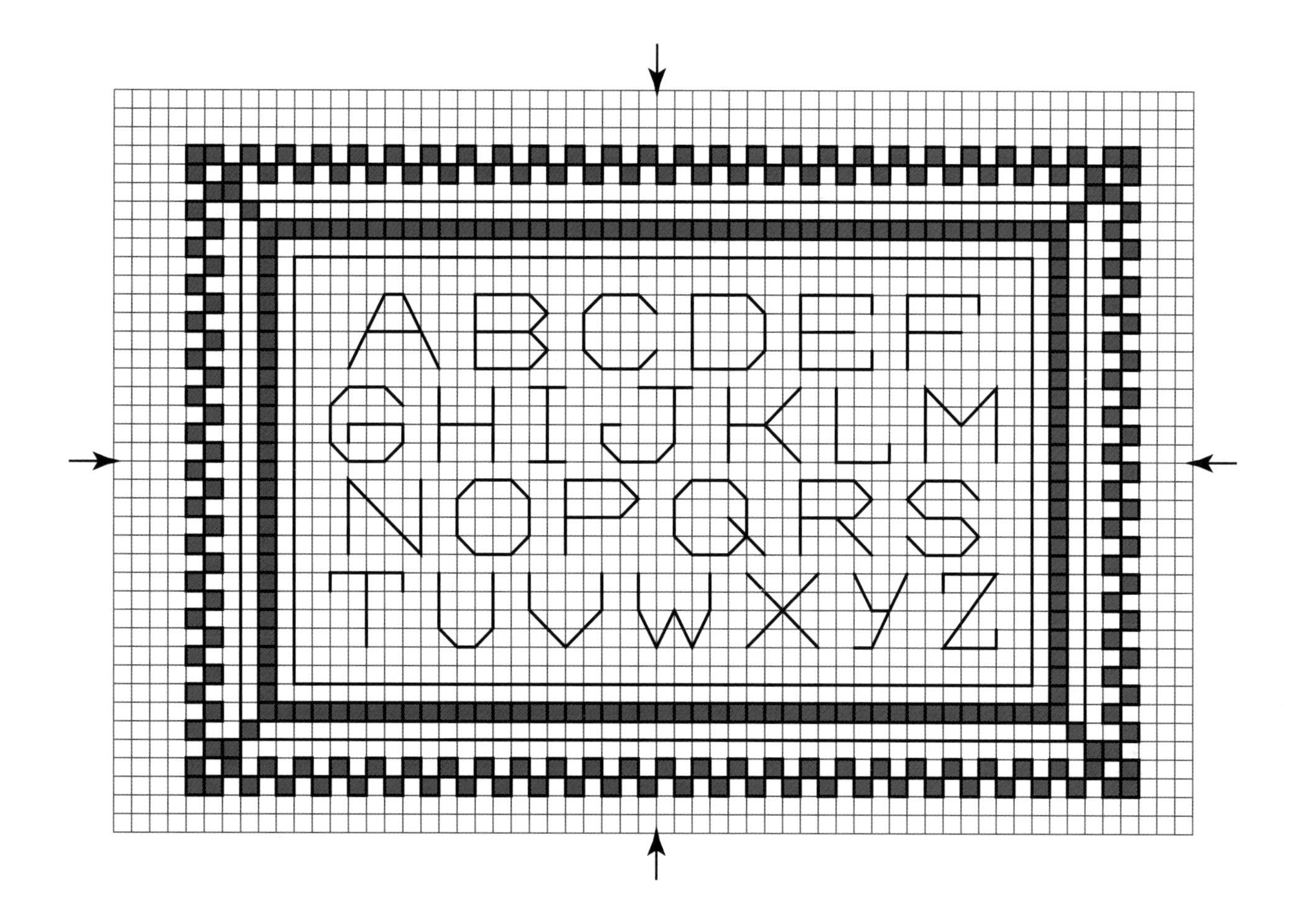

Directions

1. Fold the piece of fabric into quarters and mark the vertical and horizontal centers.
2. Using two strands of the 6-strand floss, work the cross-stitch areas, stitching one stitch over each square of fabric.
3. Using a single strand of floss, work the lines indicated in the pattern using backstitch or Holbein stitch.
4. Finish the design as a small accent cushion by trimming away the excess fabric to within an inch of the stitching. Next, cut strips of coordinating cotton quilting fabrics in random widths and stitch them to the design using all-purpose sewing thread and a ½-inch seam allowance. Add trim and finish as a pillow cover as described in the Finishing Touches chapter. Or omit the coordinating fabrics and frame the embroidery.

PROJECT 3

Antique French Sampler

SKILL LEVEL: **BEGINNER**

A classically styled design reminiscent of nineteenth-century samplers, this piece is worked in red floss. The design has two matching accessories you can stitch, a bookmark and a fob or ornament. The sampler fits a standard 6 x 6-inch frame when worked on evenweave linen.

Materials

- 20 x 20-inch piece of 22-count evenweave linen in natural or antique white
- Scraps of the same evenweave linen for the accessories
- DMC 6-strand embroidery floss in color 115 Variegated Red
- Size 24 tapestry needle

Directions

1. Fold the fabric into quarters and mark the vertical and horizontal centers.

2. Work the cross-stitch areas over two threads in the evenweave fabric using 2 strands of the 6-strand floss. Work from the center of the design outwards.

3. Frame the sampler and finish the ornament and fringed-edge bookmark as described in the Finishing Touches chapter.

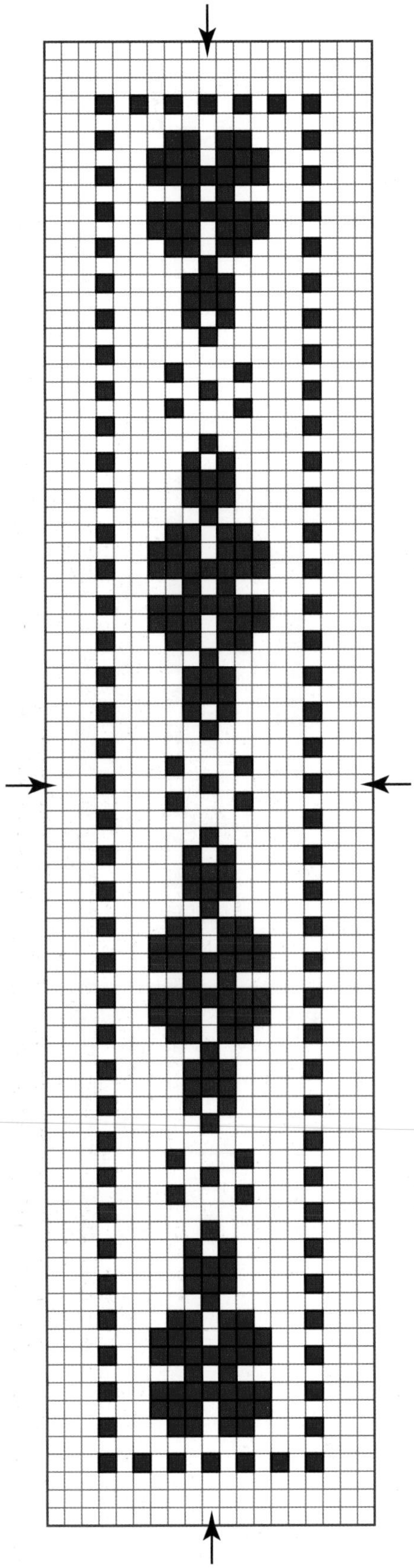

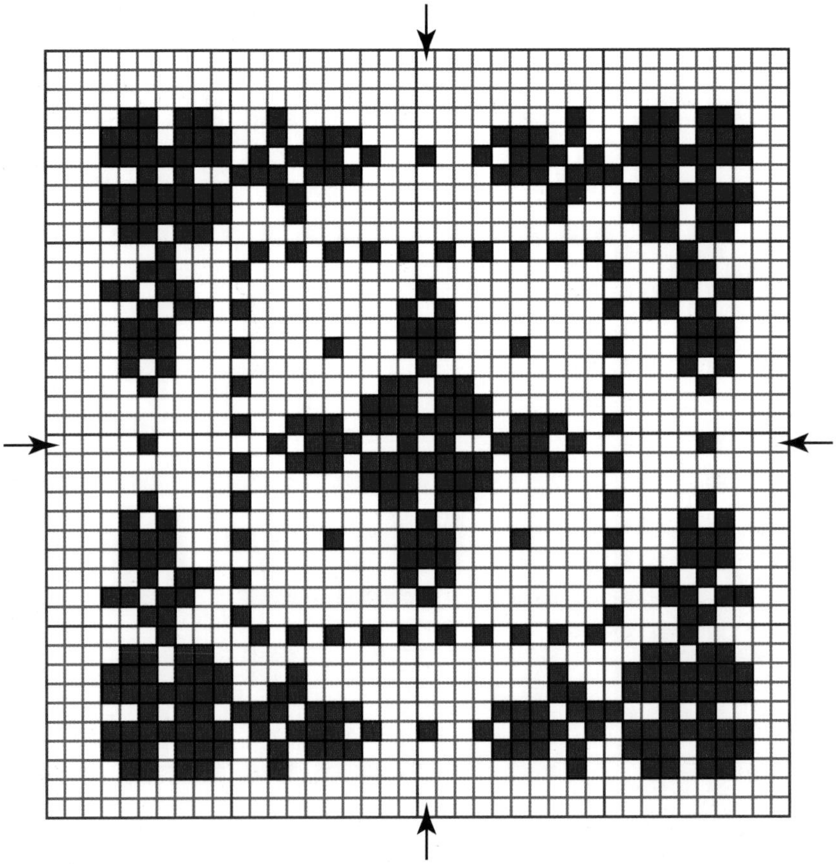

PROJECT 4

Nine Squares Sampler Pillow with Ornaments and Coaster Set

SKILL LEVEL: **INTERMEDIATE**

Nine different yet coordinating designs have been combined to make this interesting pillow. The individual squares can also be used to make a set of matching coasters and an ornament.

To stretch the designs even further, reverse the colorways, as I have done for one of the ornaments. This will give you 18 different stitching options.

Materials

- 16 x 16-inch piece of CharlesCraft 14-count Aida in White
- Scraps of the same 14-count Aida for the smaller projects
- DMC 6-strand embroidery floss in colors 645 Very Dark Beaver Gray, 834 Very Light Golden Olive, and 347 Very Dark Salmon
- Size 24 tapestry needle

Directions

PILLOW

1. Fold the 16 x 16-inch fabric into quarters and mark the vertical and horizontal centers.
2. Stitch the center block, using two strands of floss for all cross-stitch and a single strand of floss for the backstitching.
3. Work the surrounding blocks, spacing them a distance of 4 Aida squares from the center block.
4. When you have completed the stitching, trim the excess fabric 2½ inches from the outside edges of the block.
5. Finish as a pillow cover, following the directions in the Finishing Touches chapter.

COASTERS

1. Stitch one block in the center of an 8 x 8-inch scrap of the fabric.
2. Count 4 squares from the edge of the embroidery and remove the threads from row 5 around all four sides.
3. Work the hemstitch using white sewing thread in the open ditch having the anchor threads towards the embroidered center.
4. Refer to the Finishing Touches chapter for the hemstitch for making the self-fringe.

ORNAMENTS

1. Stitch one block in the center of an 8 x 8-inch scrap of the fabric.
2. Finish as described in the Finishing Touches chapter.

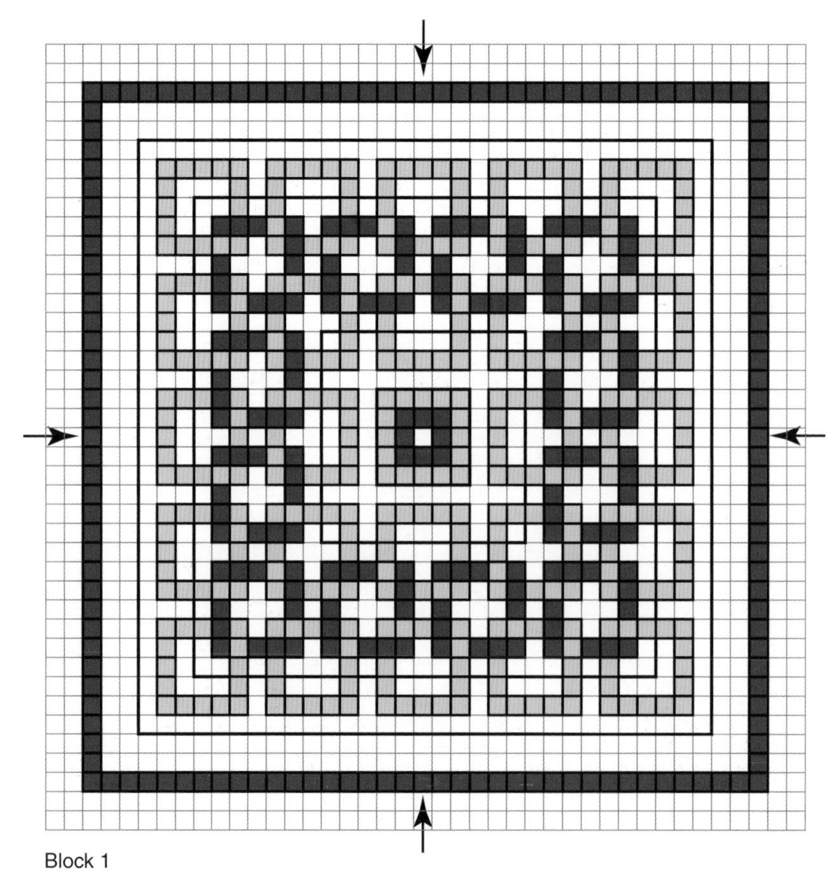

Block 1

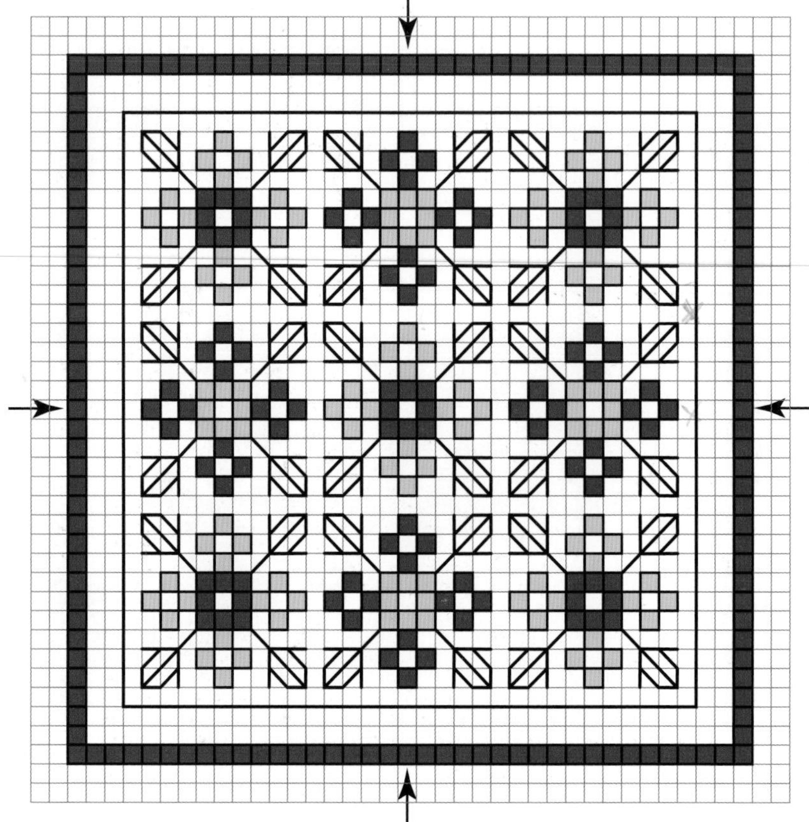

Block 2

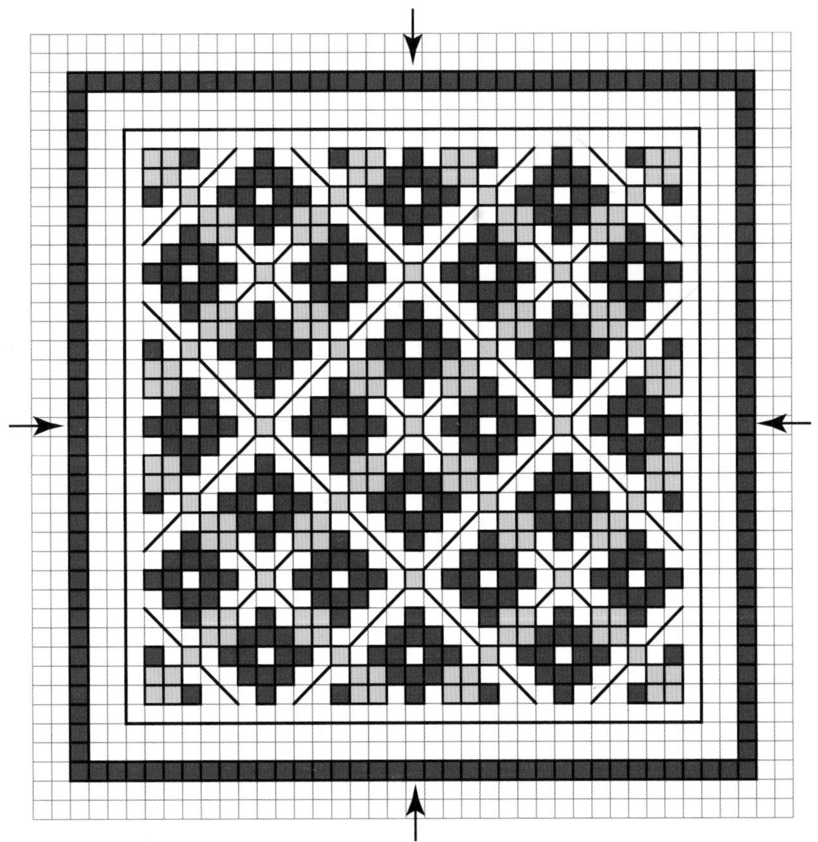

Block 3

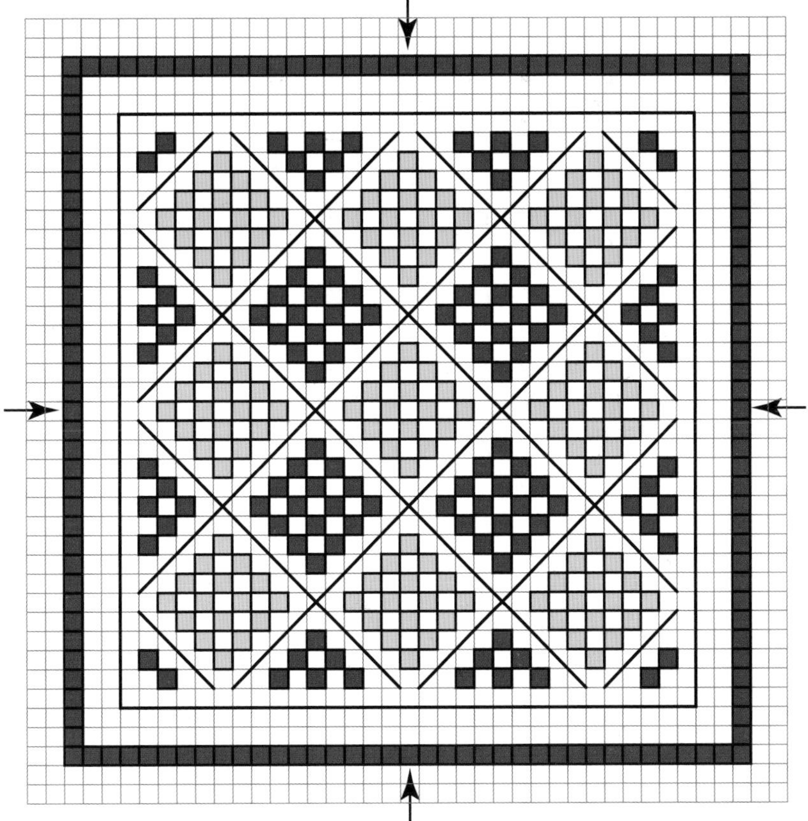

Block 4

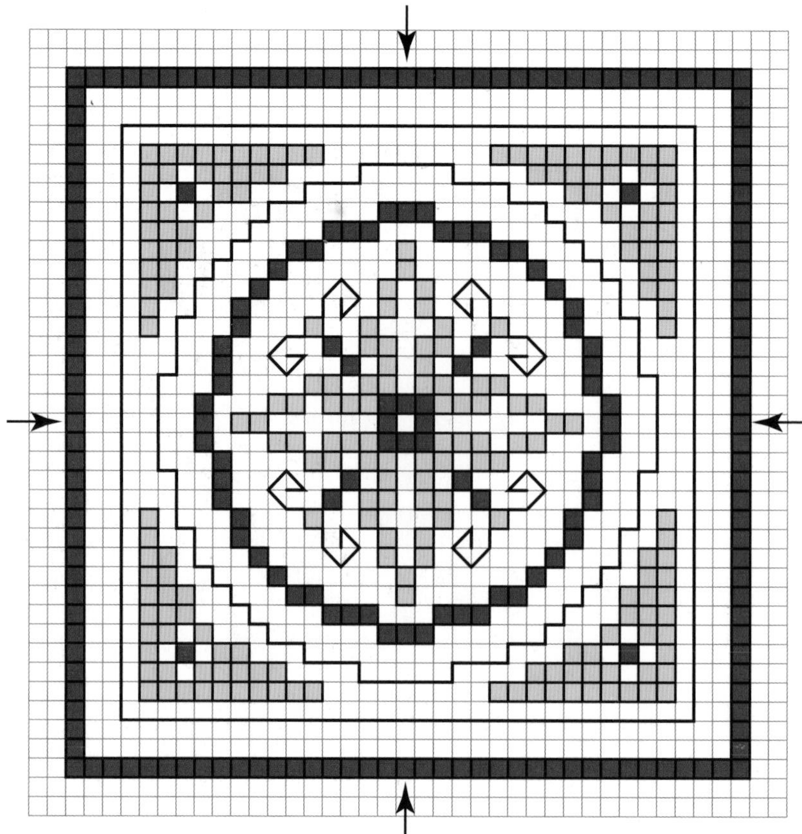

Block 5

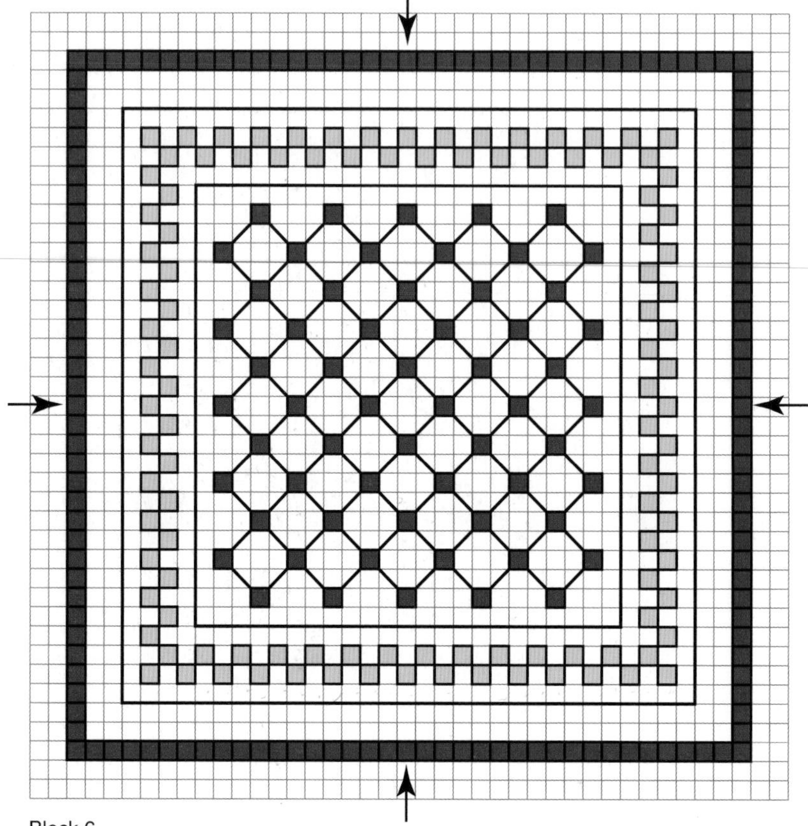

Block 6

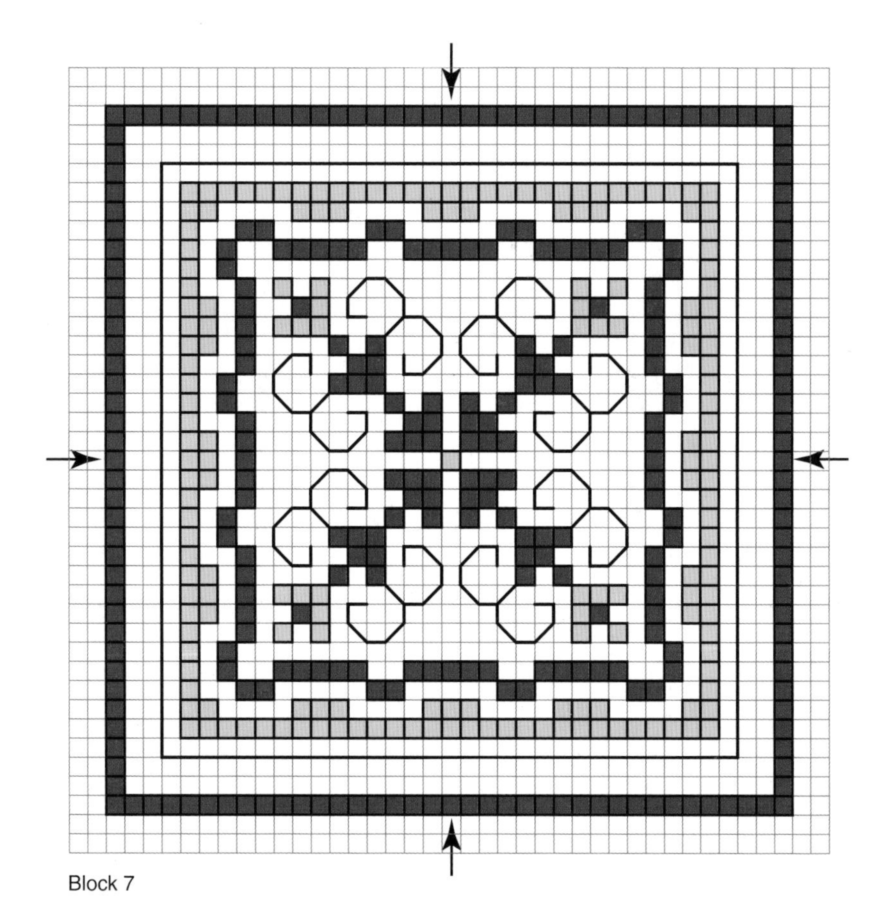

Block 7

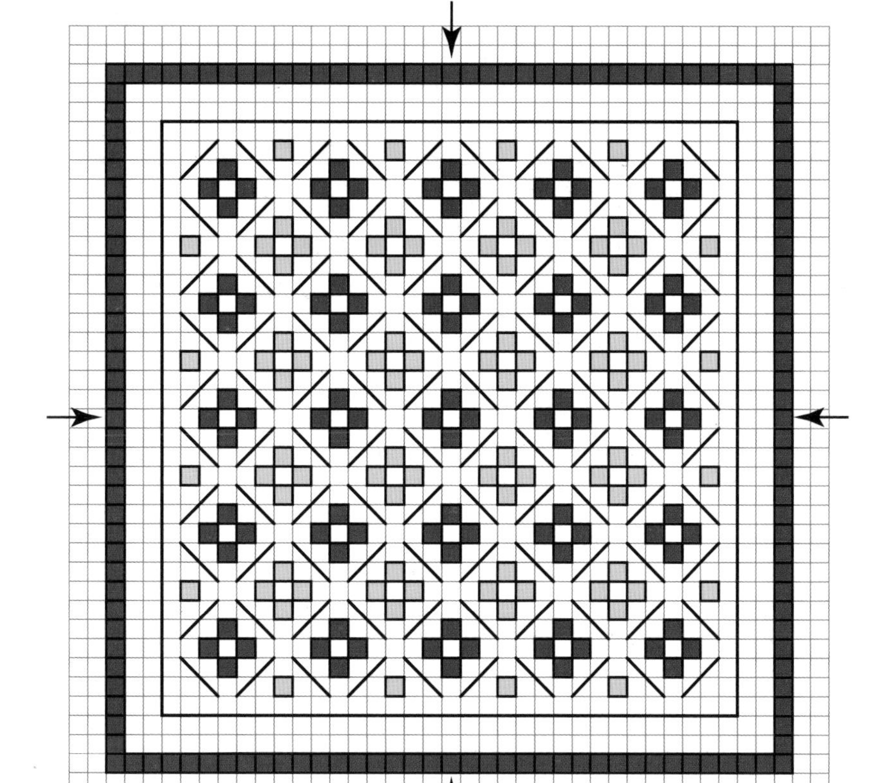

Block 8

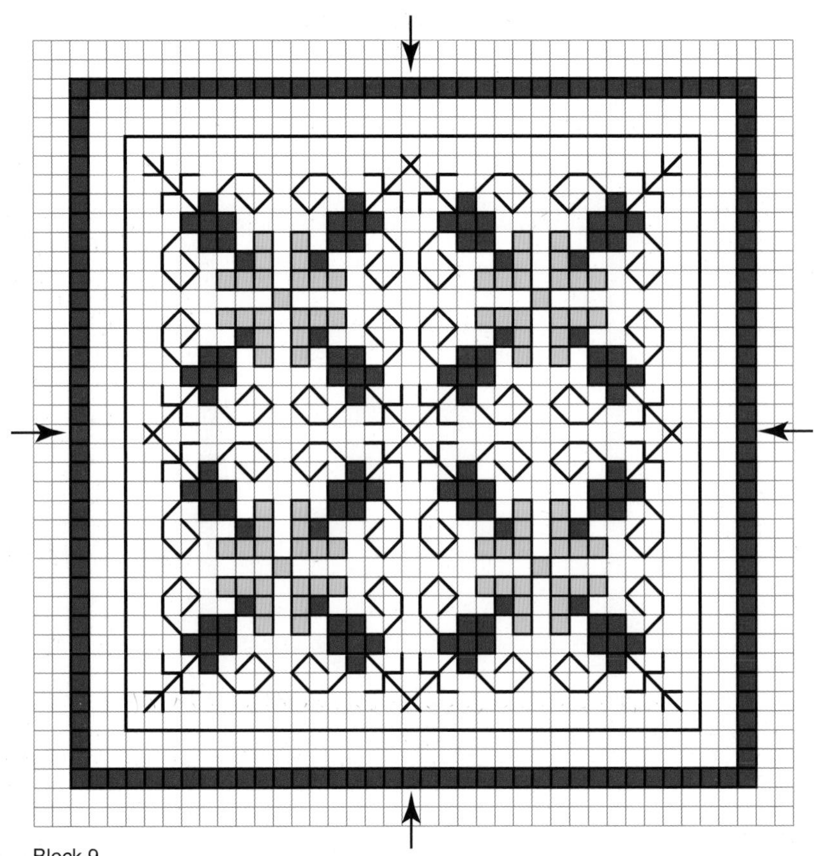

Block 9

PROJECT 5

One-Off Sampler

SKILL LEVEL: **INTERMEDIATE–ADVANCED**

This interesting sampler is not for the faint of heart and is most suitable for intermediate or advanced stitchers. In this project, you're counting over three threads in the fabric rather than the two threads you would normally when working a sampler on an evenweave fabric. Instead of the stitches covering the three threads, a thread is left unstitched between each cross-stitch, making it one off from the accompanying stitch (hence the clever name I gave this technique).

Surface embroidery stitches including stem stitch, French knots, and detached chain stitches are used for the floral sprays that enhance the alphabet. Refer to the image showing the stitching detail when working the design if you need help placing the lettering while using the one-off technique.

Materials

- CharlesCraft 20 x 24-inch Monaco fabric in White
- DMC 6-strand embroidery floss in colors 318 Light Steel Gray, 3348 Medium Teal Green, 3347 Dark Teal Green, 3821 Straw, and 970 Light Pumpkin
- Size 24 tapestry needle
- Size 10 embroidery needle

Directions

1. Fold the fabric into quarters and mark the vertical and horizontal centers.
2. Work the design as indicated in the chart, using 2 strands of the 6-strand floss.
3. Work the cross-stitch letters first, stitching from the center outwards. The spacing in between the letters will vary, but following the chart and starting a new letter where indicated will keep the design lined up in spite of the one-off stitching. This is a challenging design, but a lot of fun to stitch.
4. After the letters have been stitched, transfer the tendril markings to the fabric using a water-soluble pen or pencil. The pattern for the larger side sprays is given here full-size. Reverse the image to mark the spray on the opposite side. The smaller tendrils can be marked freehand, using the pattern as a guide.
5. Embroider the stems and tendrils in stem stitch, the leaves in detached chain stitch, and the flowers in lazy daisy stitch. A French knot is worked at the center of each flower.
6. Frame the sampler, referring to the Finishing Touches chapter.

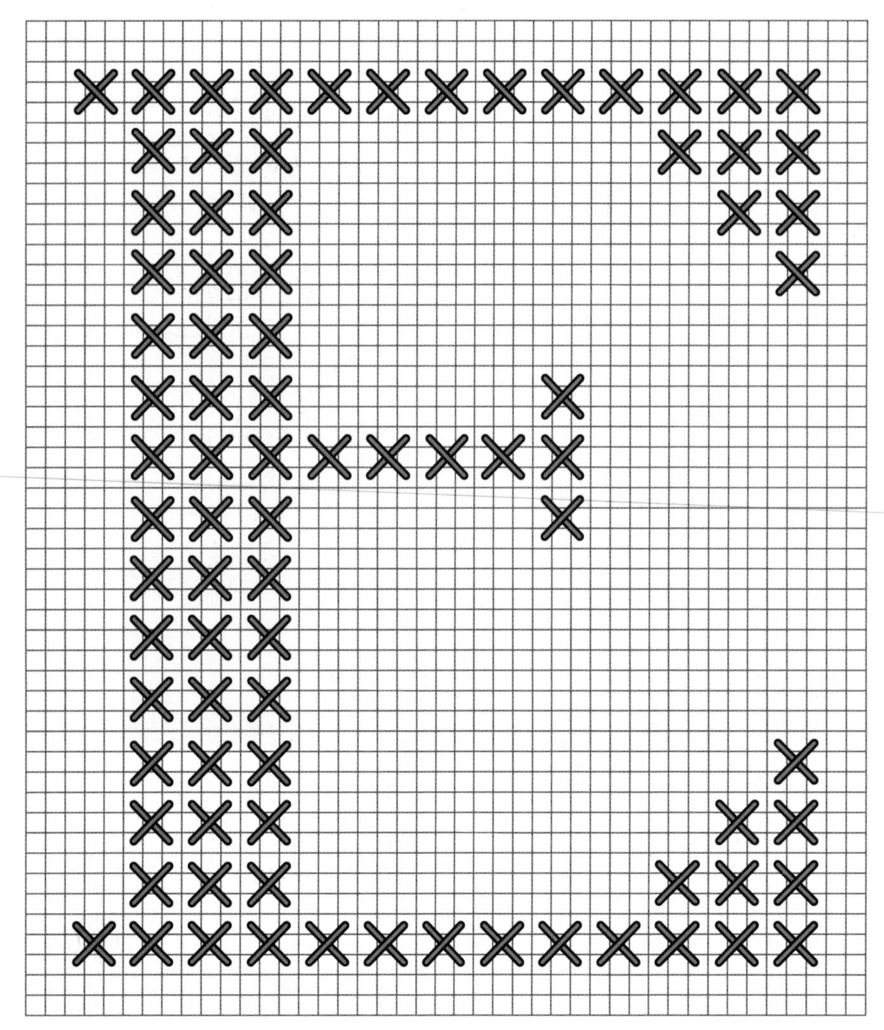

Stitching detail

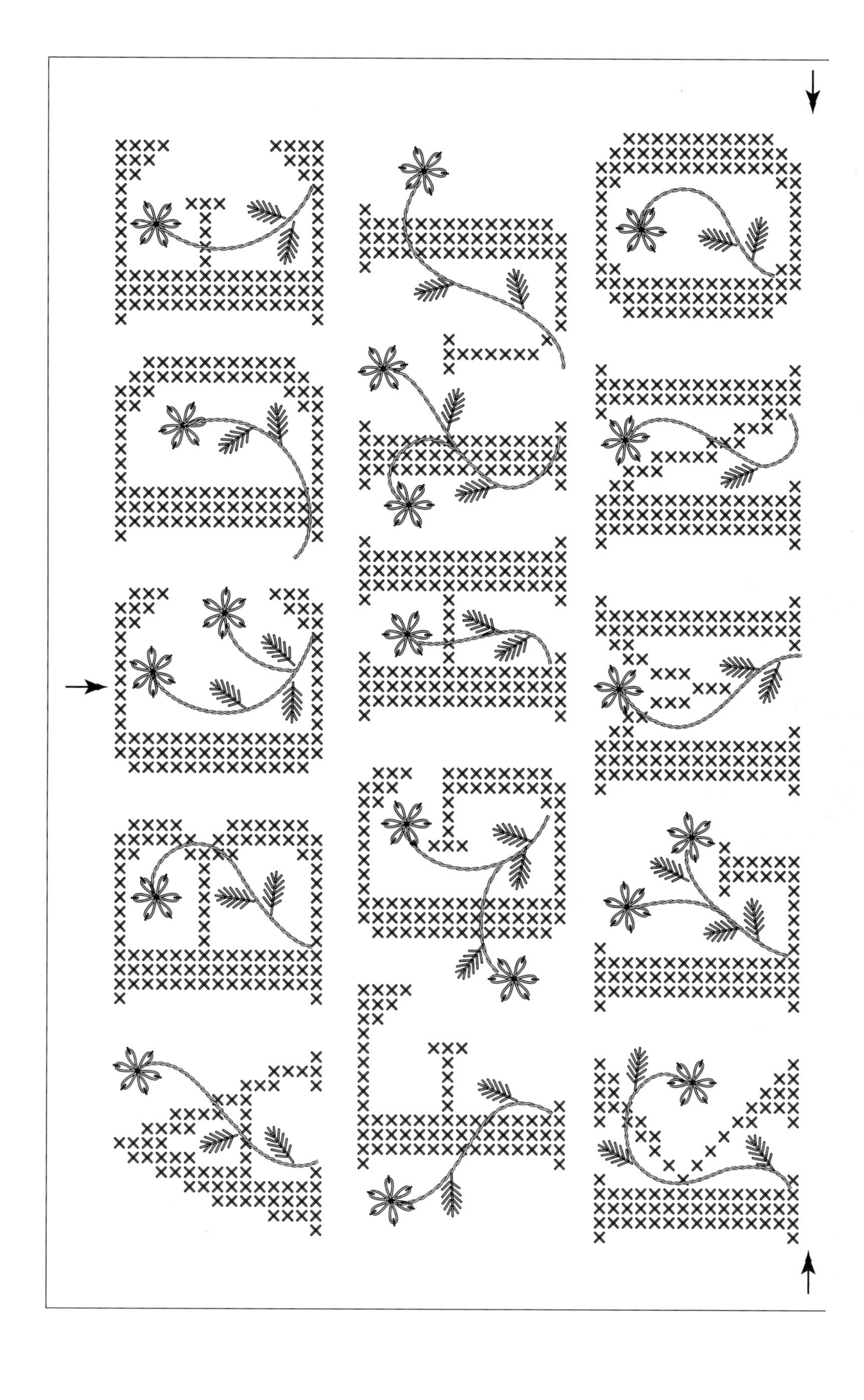

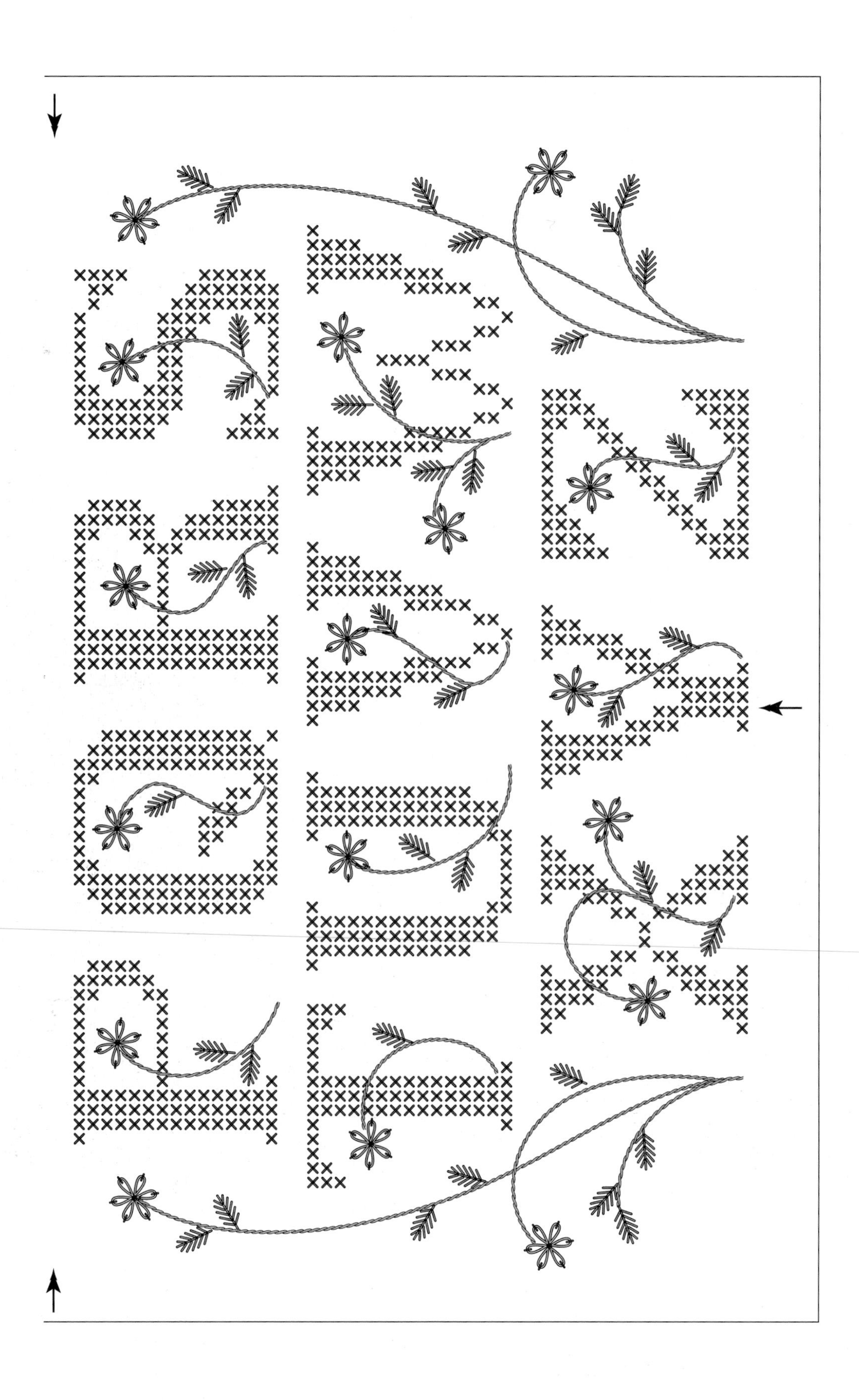

PROJECT 6

Counted-Thread Square Sampler

SKILL LEVEL: **INTERMEDIATE**

If you've ever wanted to learn basic counted-thread techniques but felt it was too difficult a task, this sampler is for you. Using just a few simple stitches, you can learn the basics of counted-thread embroidery without fear of failure.

Long (straight) stitch, counted satin stitch, fern stitch, Algerian eye, and long-armed cross-stitch are combined in a simple square pattern, using two similar colors of floss. The finished design can be framed, as shown here, or finished with the technique of your choosing.

Materials

- 10 x 10-inch piece of Zweigart 32-count Lugana Cream or Antique White
- DMC 6-strand embroidery floss in colors 738 Very Light Tan and 712 Cream
- Size 26 tapestry needle

Directions

1. Mark the vertical and horizontal centers of the evenweave fabric. Stitch from the center outward, following the graph.

   When working a chart for an evenweave design, the lines in the graph correspond to the threads in the background fabric. The stitch lines in the graph show you exactly how many threads in the fabric each stitch crosses. It's very easy and you'll have the hang of it in no time at all.
2. Detailed diagrams for each stitch are located in the Stitches chapter, but you will be able to work each of them simply by following the graph and stitching over the number of fabric threads shown.
3. Work the design by following the chart given here using 2 strands of the 6-strand floss for all stitching.
4. Frame the sampler, referring to the Finishing Touches chapter.

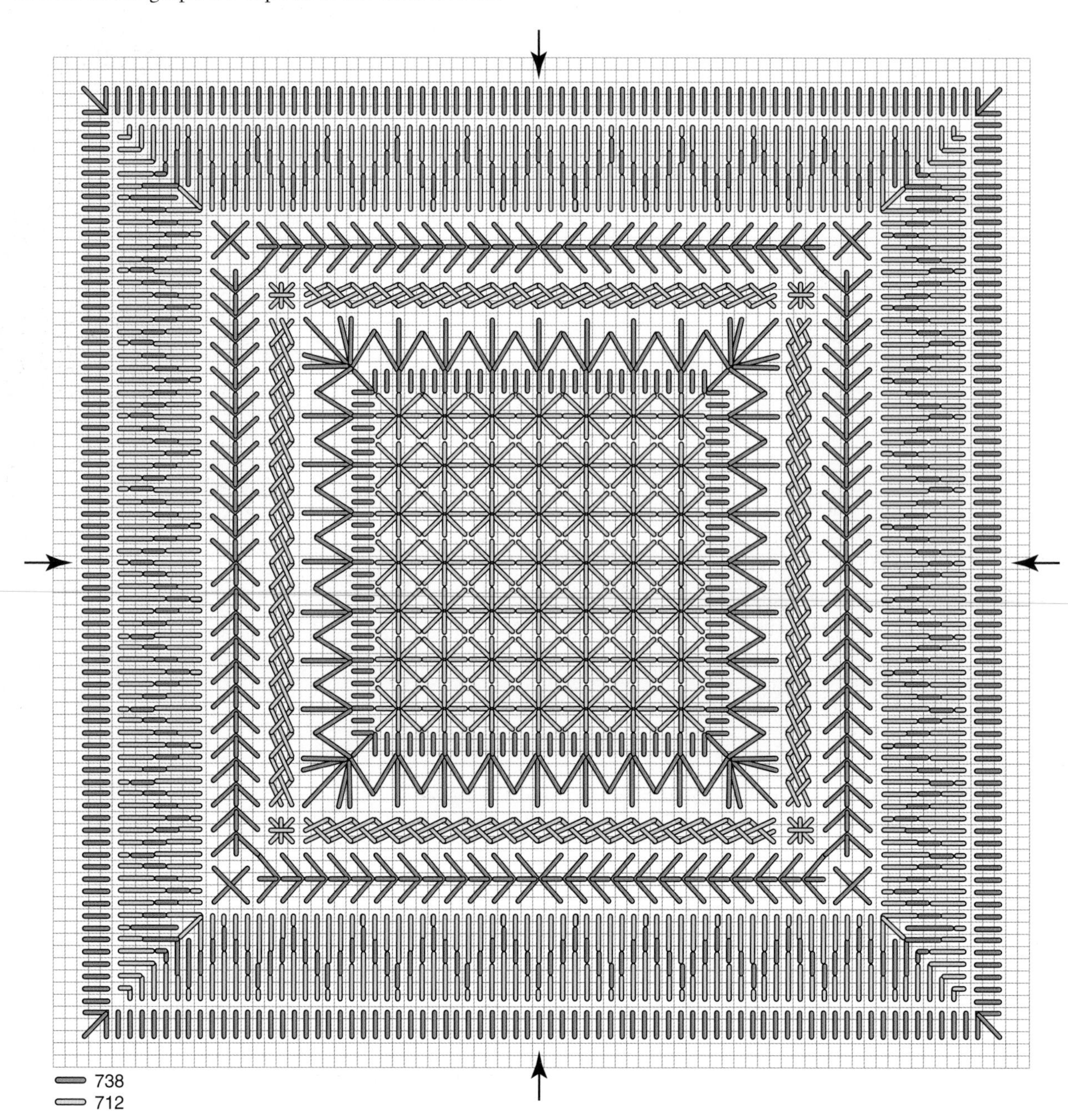

PROJECT 7

Trick or Treat Sampler

SKILL LEVEL: **BEGINNER**

Spider web festoons worked in a gorgeous metallic thread, beaded eyes on the spiders, and variegated thread give this sampler worked on Aida cloth a bit of Halloween drama. Designed to fit a square frame with a 10 x 10-inch opening, the sampler is quick to work and makes a nice addition to your boo-tiful Halloween décor.

Materials

- 20 x 20-inch piece of white or off-white Aida
- DMC 6-strand embroidery floss in colors 51 Variegated Orange, 310 Black, and 907 Light Parrot Green
- DMC Light Effects Floss color 317 Titanium
- Size 11/0 glass seed beads, orange
- Size 24 tapestry needle
- Beading needle

Directions

1. Fold the fabric into quarters and mark the vertical and horizontal centers.
2. Work the design from the center outwards using 2 strands of floss for all cross-stitches. When working the spider web areas, use a single strand of the light effects floss in backstitch and straight stitch. Note that these are longer stitches that cross over more than one square of the fabric.
3. When the stitching has been completed, attach the beads using a single strand of the orange floss and the beading needle. Two beads are needed for each spider and a single bead is attached to the center outside edge of each spider web festoon.
4. Frame the sampler, referring to the Finishing Touches chapter.

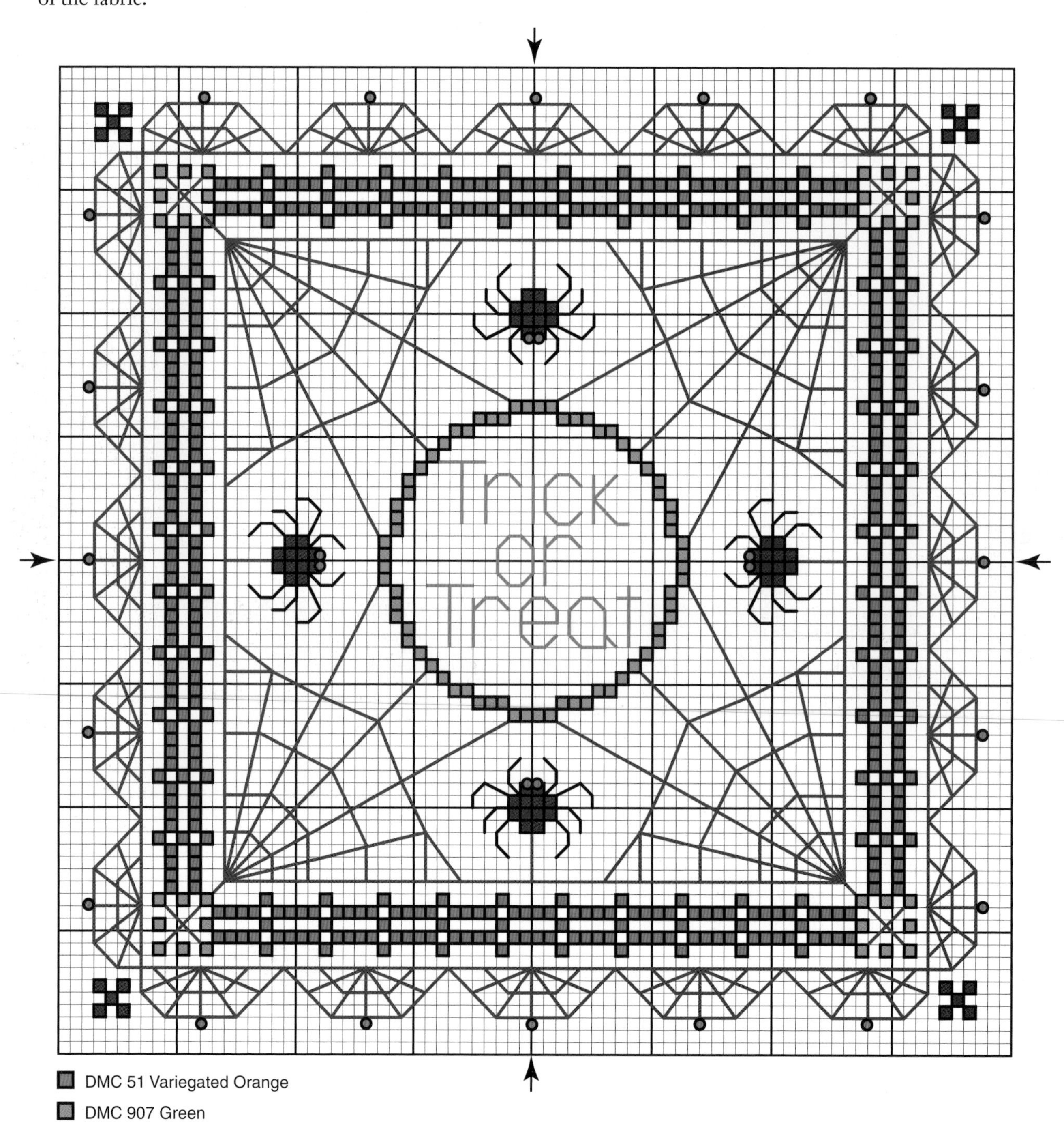

- DMC 51 Variegated Orange
- DMC 907 Green
- DMC 310 Black
- DMC Light Effects E317
- Orange seed beed

PROJECT 8
Counted-Thread Band Sampler

SKILL LEVEL: **BEGINNER**

Stitch this band sampler as a testimonial of all the embroidery stitches you have learned. Each band in the design features bright, colorful threads worked in surface embroidery stitches or composite stitches across the width of the fabric. Use the same colors and stitches shown here, or select your own colors and vary the stitches or the size of the finished design. Anything goes with a band sampler!

Materials

- 18 x 18-inch piece of 28-count white CharlesCraft Lugana
- 9 x 9-inch ready-made frame
- DMC 6-strand embroidery floss in colors 553 Violet, 554 Light Violet, 726 Light Topaz, 760 Salmon, 954 Nile Green, and 3853 Dark Autumn Gold
- DMC Color Variations 6-strand embroidery floss in colors 4022 Mediterranean Sea, 4030 Monet's Garden, 4050 Roaming Pastures, 4126 Desert Canyon, and 4190 Ocean Coral
- Size 24 tapestry needle

Directions

1. Fold the fabric into quarters and mark the vertical center.
2. Measure 5 inches upwards from the horizontal center and mark. This will be the top line. You'll start in the center top and work down.

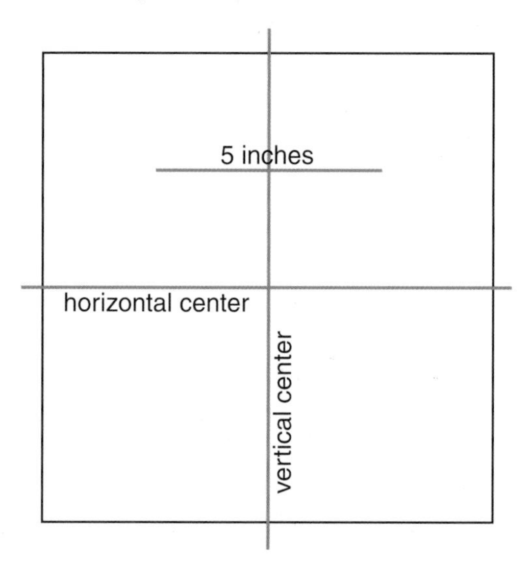

3. Referring to the charts, work the designs from the center line out towards the edges. Each band of stitching should measure close to 10 inches in width. The charts for this sampler (on the next 3 pages) are counted-thread charts, which means that each line in the chart corresponds to one warp or weft thread in the fabric, and stitches are worked between and over a designated number of threads in the fabric.
4. Each chart contains several rows of bands showing how each stitch is worked on the evenweave fabric, but you can also refer to the Stitches chapter for additional information on working each stitch. Stitches used in this project include counted satin stitch, backstitch, cross-stitch, fly stitch, fern stitch, double chevron, star stitch, detached chain, French knots, feather stitch, ermine stitch, Chinese cross-stitch, tied gobelin, upright cross, and combinations of stitches. Feel free to mix them up if desired, as this band sampler is meant to have a freeform look.
5. Frame the sampler, referring to the Finishing Touches chapter.

Part 1

Part 2

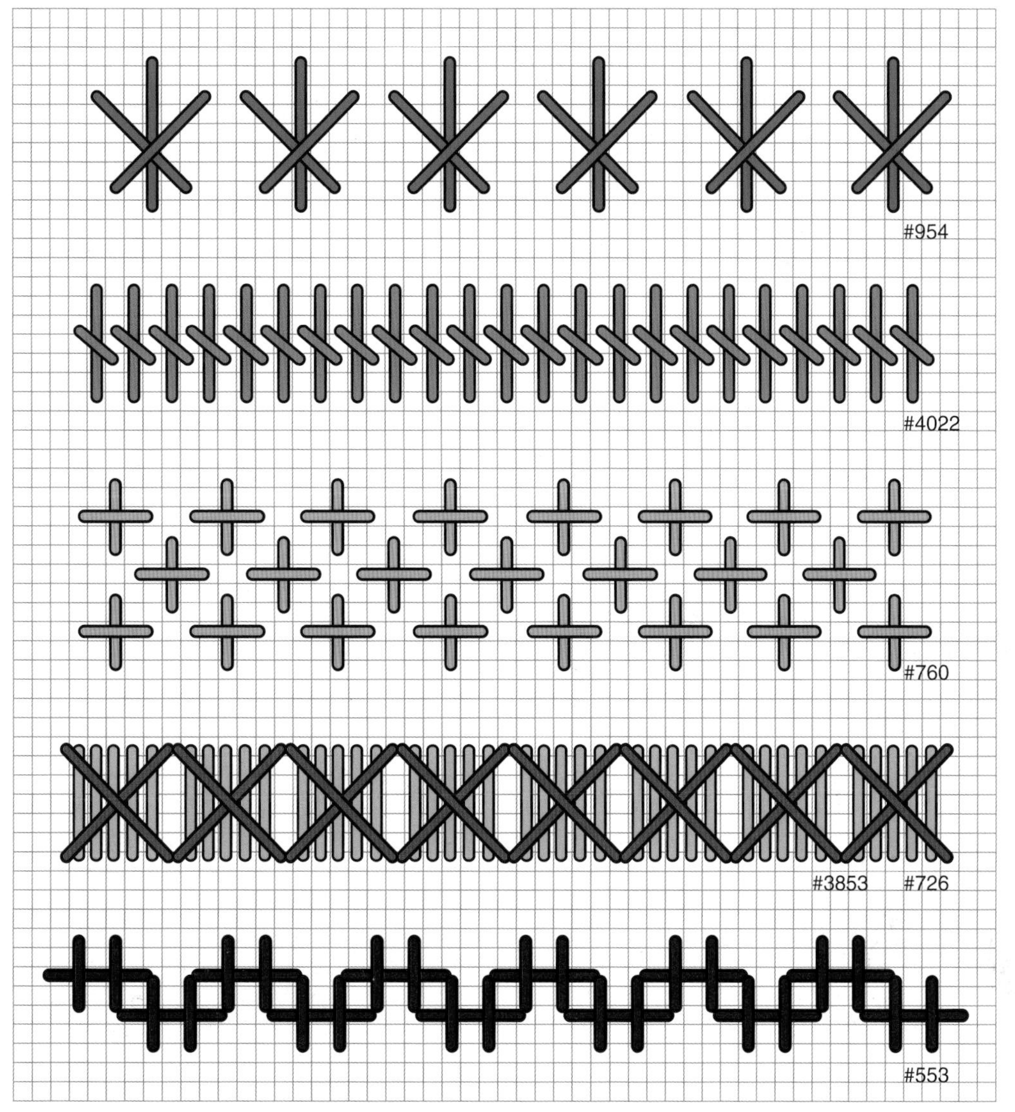

Part 3

PROJECT 9
Christmas Balls Sampler and Pillow Set

SKILL LEVEL: **INTERMEDIATE**

Looking for a project that will keep you busy for a while? This cross-stitch sampler with counted-thread borders will definitely do the trick. Although the sampler isn't difficult, it is time-consuming to create, with each ball ornament composed of 363 individual stitches. The project calls for 25 different colors of thread, so you'll need a large project bag.

If you're pressed for time, you can make the matching pillow using just four of the lettered balls to spell NOEL, or use the balls to spell out any holiday sentiment you wish: JOY, CHEER, or WELCOME are just a few ideas for coordinating projects.

Materials

- 20 x 24-inch piece of 28-count DMC Monaco fabric in white for sampler
- 14 x 20-inch piece of the same fabric for the pillow
- DMC 6-strand embroidery floss in colors 3857 Dark Rosewood, 304 Medium Red, 817 Very Dark Coral Red, 3844 Dark Bright Turquoise, 3845 Medium Bright Turquoise, 747 Very Light Sky Blue, 972 Deep Canary, 725 Medium Light Topaz, 727 Very Light Topaz, 154 Very Dark Grape, 552 Medium Violet, 210 Medium Lavender, 905 Dark Parrot Green, 704 Bright Chartreuse, 472 Ultra Light Avadodo Green, 335 Rose, 957 Pale Geranium, 818 Baby Pink, 350 Medium Coral, 352 Light Coral, 754 Light Peach, B5200 Snow White, 505 Jade Green, and 3862 Dark Mocha Beige
- DMC Light Effects embroidery floss in 3852 Dark Gold
- Size 24 tapestry needle

Directions

1. Fold the fabric into quarters and mark the vertical and horizontal centers.
2. Work the alphabet balls in cross-stitch over 2 threads in the fabric, working from the center outwards and using 2 strands of floss.
3. Work the gold metal tops in cross-stitch using 2 strands of the gold metallic thread. Use a single strand of the metallic gold floss and backstitch for the hanging loop of each ball.
4. Work the branches between the balls in backstitch using two strands of floss and color 3862.
5. Work the pine needles in straight stitch using 2 strands of color 505.
6. Frame the sampler or finish the pillow as described in the Finishing Touches chapter.

Color Key
905
704
472
3857
304
817
3844
3846
747
972
725
727
335
957
818
154
552
210
350
352
754
Gold metallic
B5200
505
3862

C
D
H
I
J

Color Key
905
704
472
3857
304
817
3844
3846
747
972
725
727
335
957
818
154
552
210
350
352
754
Gold metallic
B5200
505
3862

Color Key

905
3857
3844
972
335
154
350
Gold metallic
704
304
3846
725
957
552
352
B5200
472
817
747
727
818
210
754
505
3862

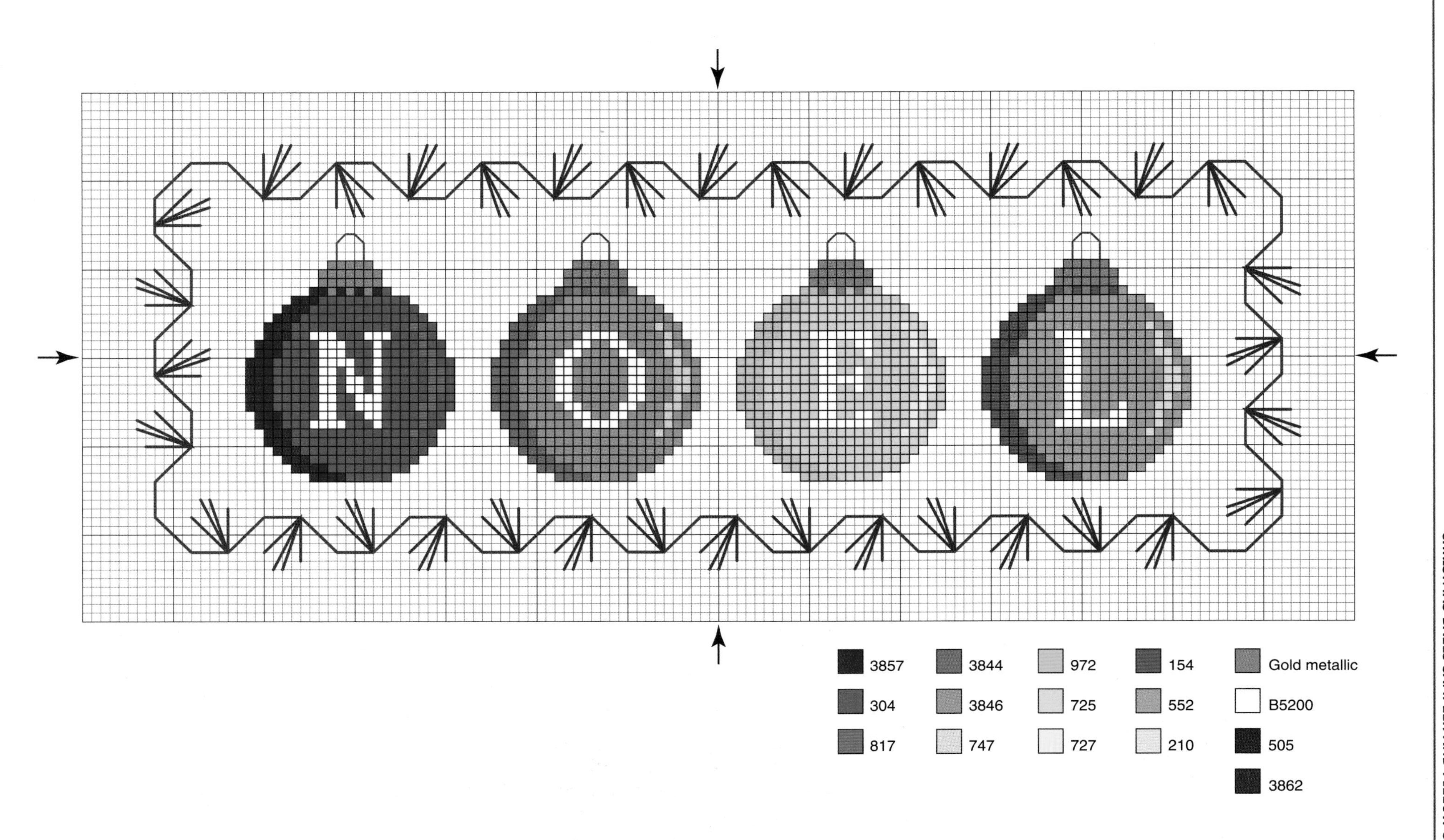
3857
3844
972
154
Gold metallic
304
3846
725
552
B5200
817
747
727
210
505
3862

PROJECT 10

Hanukkah Sampler

SKILL LEVEL: **INTERMEDIATE–ADVANCED**

Here's a small-scale design that can be worked up quickly, using just two colors of thread, and finished with a fringed edge. The completed project can be used as a mat to display your favorite dreidel, used as a coaster for drinks, or framed on a color mat for display. Gold seed beads add a touch of glitz to this project, which utilizes a variety of easy counted-thread stitches.

Materials

- 16 x 16-inch piece of 28-count DMC Monaco fabric in white or natural
- DMC 6-strand embroidery floss in colors 312 Very Dark Baby Blue and 3755 Baby Blue
- Size 11/0 glass seed beads, gold
- Size 24 tapestry needle
- Beading needle

Directions

1. Mark the horizontal and vertical centers of the even-weave fabric.

2. Stitch the design, following the chart. Work from the center outwards and use 2 strands of the 6-strand floss for all stitching. The lines in the chart correspond to the threads in the background fabric. The stitch lines in the graph show you how many threads in the fabric each stitch crosses. Stitches used include running stitch, straight stitch, cross-stitch and long-armed cross-stitch. The chart below is enlarged, making it easier to see the detail in each stitched area.

3. When you have finished working all four quarters, the piece will look like the image on page 52.

4. Stitch the seed beads in place using after working the embroidery, using the beading needle and a single strand of the light blue floss.

5. If fringing the edge, count out 14 threads in the fabric and pull out the 15th thread around all 4 sides. Work the hemstitch with the light blue floss in the open ditch, having the anchor threads towards the embroidered center. Stitch a row of running stitch, 1 thread in, just inside the hemstitched area.

6. Finish the sampler, following the directions in the Finishing Touches chapter for making a self-fringed edge.

Full view

PROJECT 11
Pineapple Sampler

SKILL LEVEL: **BEGINNER**

The pineapple has long been used as a symbol of hospitality, and in this sampler it is used to welcome guests in a simple wall hanging worked in autumn colors. The design works up quickly using cross-stitch and backstitch in just four colors of embroidery floss. The finished project makes a beautiful housewarming gift for a new neighbor.

Materials

- 15 x 18-inch piece of CharlesCraft Fiddlers Cloth Aida in Light Oatmeal
- DMC 6-strand embroidery floss in colors 3830 Terra Cotta, 730 Very Dark Olive Green, 734 Light Olive Green, and 3820 Dark Straw
- Size 24 tapestry needle

Directions

1. Fold the fabric into quarters and mark the vertical and horizontal centers.
2. Following the chart and the color key, work the cross-stitch areas from the center of the design outwards, using 2 strands of the 6-strand floss. Work the back-stitched areas using a single strand of floss. The tendrils can be worked in Holbein stitch using a single strand of floss if you prefer.
3. Frame the sampler, or finish as a large ornament with a cardboard insert instead of fiberfill stuffing, as I have done in the sample. Refer to the Finishing Touches chapter for instructions.

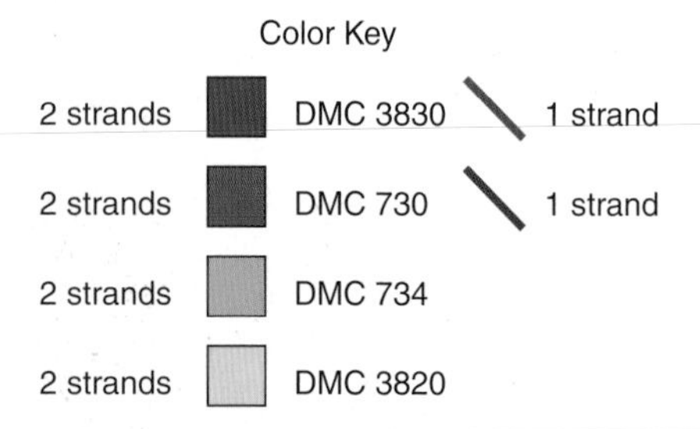

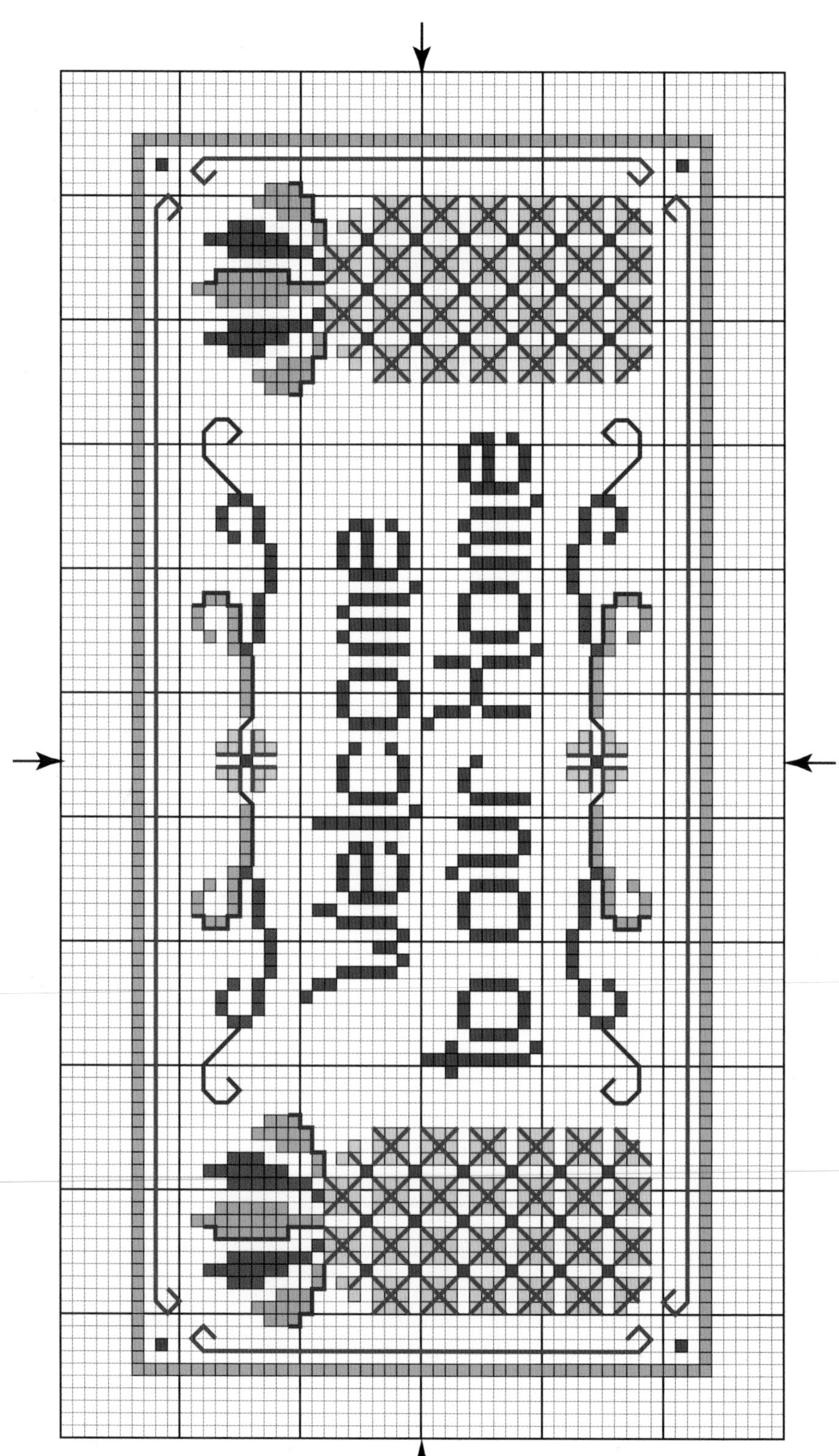

PROJECT 12

Schoolhouse Sampler

SKILL LEVEL: **BEGINNER**

Surface embroidery stitches also can be used to make samplers, as I've done in this project that utilizes basic embroidery stitches, including backstitch, lazy daisy stitch, and French knots. Additional color is optional and can be added after the stitching has been completed using wax-based colored pencils.

The pattern has been designed to fit a standard 8½ x 11-inch document frame, making it ideal as a gift for a favorite teacher or to display in your home to celebrate back-to-school season.

Materials

- 16 x 18-inch piece of natural-color plainweave broadcloth or other densely woven fabric
- DMC 6-strand embroidery floss in colors 321 Red, 3820 Dark Straw, 535 Very Light Ash Gray, 906 Medium Parrot Green, 3818 Ultra Very Dark Emerald Green, 420 Dark Hazelnut Brown, and 517 Dark Wedgewood Blue
- Size 10 embroidery needle
- Colored pencils in at least two shades each of blue, green, red, yellow, and brown (optional)

1 2 3
SCHOOL
A B C

Directions

1. Transfer the design onto the fabric using the water-soluble fabric marking pen, centering the design on the fabric. If you have difficulty seeing the pattern through the fabric, use a light box or trace the design by holding the fabric and pattern up to a window.

2. Embroider the design using 3 strands of the 6-strand embroidery floss throughout. The schoolhouse, berries in the outer shrubs, and hearts are worked in red; the roof and interior windows in dark straw; the lettering, bell, and steps to the schoolhouse in ash gray; the door, star, leaves next to the hearts, and shrubs in the two shades of green; the sign over the schoolhouse door and the border in brown; and the birds, window frames, and flowers in blue.

3. All of the stitching has been worked in backstitch, with the following exceptions: the berries in the outer bushes and the eyes of the birds, which have been worked in French knots; the flowers in the inner bushes, which have been worked in lazy daisy stitch; and the leaves next to the hearts, which have been worked in detached chain stitch.

4. Once the embroidery has been completed, prepare the fabric for coloring by washing out the marking pen or pencil, and press the piece while still damp. Refer to the Basic Techniques chapter for instructions on using colored pencils in a project. Color the inside areas of the motifs in the design.

5. Refer to the Finishing Touches chapter for basic framing instructions.

PROJECT 13
Seasonal Samplers

SKILL LEVEL: **BEGINNER**

Make a set of four seasonal samplers worked in a variety of surface embroidery stitches. The four different designs—one each for spring, winter, summer, and autumn—can each be framed, or you can use one frame and simply change the insert with the seasons. You might also want to stitch the four motifs into a little wall quilt, as the motifs are made to fit an 8 x 8-inch block.

Materials

- 16 x 18-inch piece of natural-colored plainweave broadcloth or other densely woven fabric
- DMC 6-strand embroidery floss in colors 209 Dark Lavender, 434 Light Brown, 470 Light Avocado Green, 517 Dark Wedgewood, 518 Light Wedgewood, 603 Cranberry, 721 Medium Orange Spice, 732 Olive Green, 733 Medium Olive Green, 783 Medium Topaz, 799 Medium Delft Blue, and 920 Medium Copper
- Size 10 embroidery needle

Directions

1. Transfer the design onto the fabric using the water-soluble fabric marking pen, centering the design on the fabric. If you have difficulty seeing the pattern through the fabric, use a light box or trace the design by holding the fabric and pattern up to a window.
2. Embroider the design using 2 strands of the 6-strand embroidery floss throughout, following the color key. Solid lines are worked in stem stitch, dashed lines in running stitch, large dots in French knots, and flowers and leaves in lazy daisy or detached chain stitches.
3. When you have completed the embroidery and washed out the markings, mount each design on a piece of foam-core board cut to fit the inside dimensions of an 8 x 8-inch frame. Refer to the Finishing Touches chapter for instructions. Change the insert with the seasons.

Spring Color Key

- 518
- 603
- 733
- 209
- 783
- 434

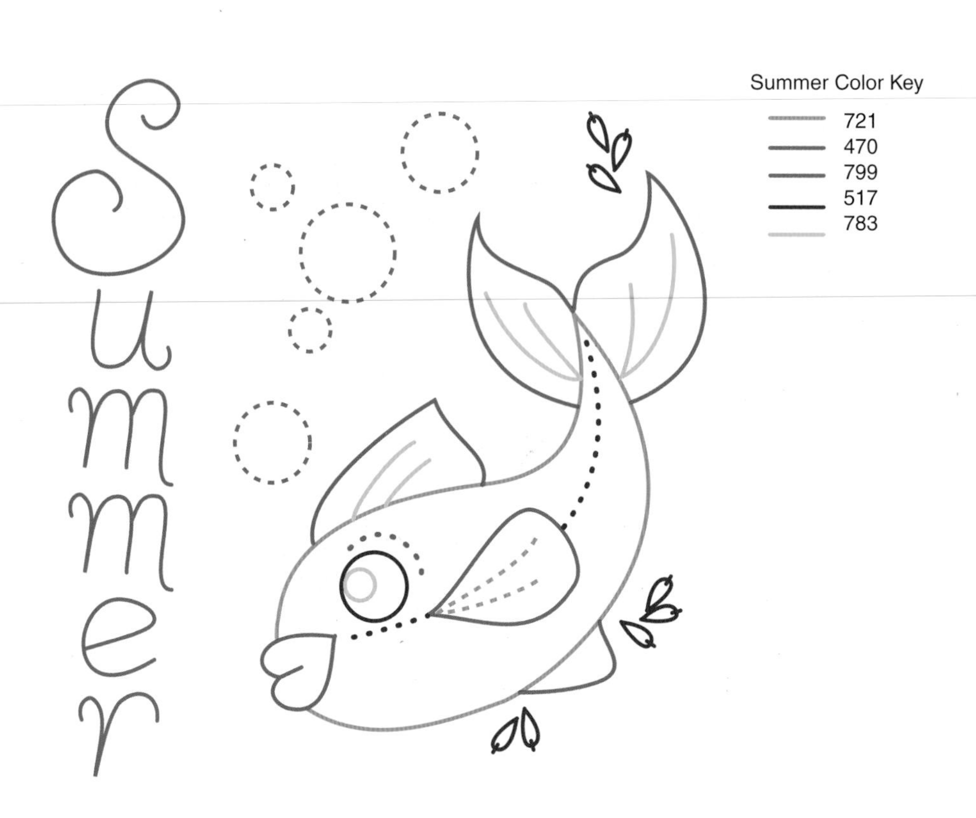

Summer Color Key

- 721
- 470
- 799
- 517
- 783

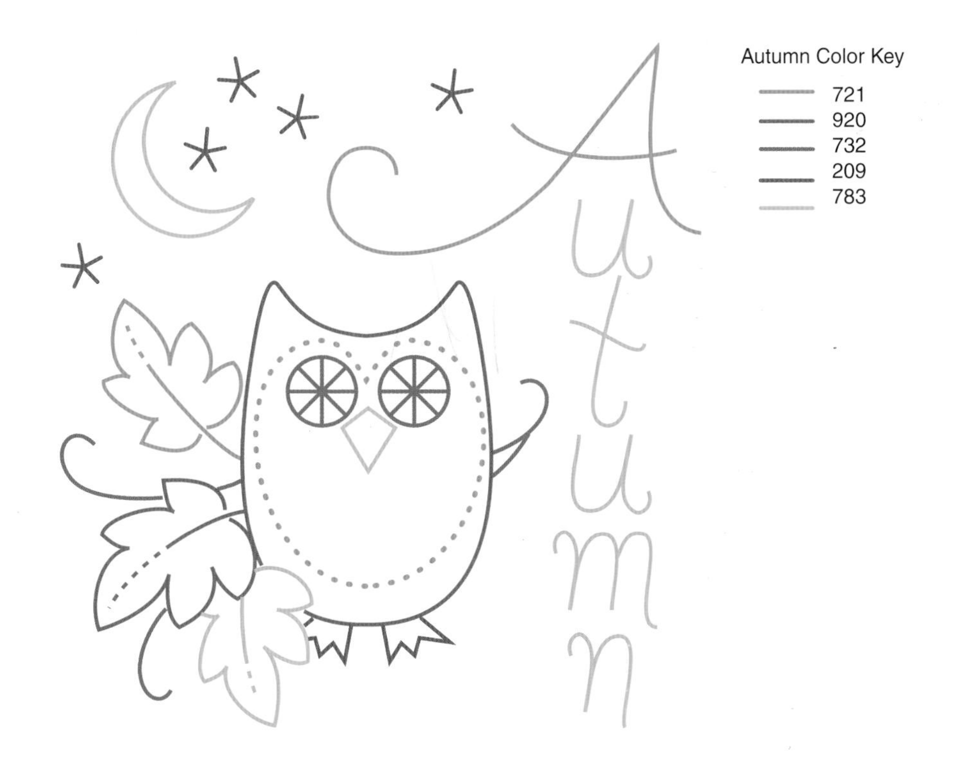
Autumn
Autumn Color Key
721
920
732
209
783

Winter
Winter Color Key
517
783
470
209
434

Autumn

Spring

Summer

Winter

PROJECT 14
Shamrock Sampler

SKILL LEVEL: **BEGINNER-INTERMEDIATE**

This delicate, lacy sampler is worked in just one color of embroidery floss using basic embroidery stitches. The variegated green floss keeps the use of a single color from being boring, and tiny glass seed beads add sparkle. The design here is sized to fit a 10-inch frame, but can be easily enlarged or reduced to fit any square frame.

Materials

- 18 x 18-inch piece of natural-colored plainweave broadcloth or other densely woven fabric
- DMC Color Variations 6-strand embroidery floss in color 4047 Princess Garden
- Size 11/0 glass seed beads, green
- Size 10 embroidery needle
- Beading needle

Directions

1. Transfer the design onto the fabric using the water-soluble fabric marking pen, centering the design on the fabric. If you have difficulty seeing the pattern through the fabric, use a light box or trace the design by holding the fabric and pattern up to a window.
2. Embroider the design using 2 strands of the 6-strand embroidery floss throughout.
3. Work the solid lines in stem stitch and use running stitch for the dashed lines. Use detached chain stitch to work the smaller flowers and the small leaves that are sprouting along the tendrils in the design. A full lazy daisy is stitched at the center of the design.
4. The small dots on the pattern indicate the placement of the seed beads. Stitch them in place using a single strand of the floss and the beading needle. Use one seed bead per dot. French knots can be worked in these areas instead, if desired, using 2 strands of floss.

PROJECT 15

Smile and Be Happy Sampler

SKILL LEVEL: **BEGINNER**

This uplifting sampler is made to fit a ready-made 5 x 7-inch frame. It's the perfect piece to grace your office or cubicle and will surely brighten up your outlook on *one of those days*. I've stitched the design using a bright happy shade of orange in equally happy over-dyed floss. It just screams of sunshine, citrus, and sorbet. What could be happier than that?

Materials

- 8 x 10-inch piece of white plainweave broadcloth or other densely woven fabric
- DMC Color Variations 6-strand embroidery floss in color 4124 Bonfire
- Size 10 embroidery needle

Directions

1. Transfer the design onto the fabric using the water-soluble fabric marking pen, centering the design on the fabric. If you have difficulty seeing the pattern through the fabric, use a light box or trace the design by holding the fabric and pattern up to a window.
2. Embroider the design using 2 strands of the 6-strand embroidery floss throughout.
3. Work the lines in backstitch, the tiny little leaves in detached chain stitch, and the flowers in lazy daisy stitch.
4. After removing the markings, work a single French knot at the center of each flower, or add a small button or bead to embellish the project.

PROJECT 16

Pumpkins on the Square

SKILL LEVEL: **BEGINNER–INTERMEDIATE**

Stitch this square design and finish as a framed piece of art, a pillow, or the focal point of a quilted wall hanging. The simple design is repeated diagonally on all four corners with a central motif, but you can also use the motifs individually for even more versatility. Feel free to substitute French knots for the beads, if desired.

Materials

- 16 x 16-inch piece of white plainweave broadcloth or other densely woven fabric
- DMC 6-strand embroidery floss in colors 3828 Hazelnut Brown, 3852 Very Dark Straw, 471 Very Light Avocado Green, 469 Avocado Green, 740 Tangerine, and 720 Dark Orange Spice
- Size 10 embroidery needle
- Size 11/0 glass seed beads, orange
- Beading needle

Directions

1. Transfer the design onto the fabric using the water-soluble fabric marking pen, centering the design on the fabric. If you have difficulty seeing the pattern through the fabric, use a light box or trace the design by holding the fabric and pattern up to a window.
2. Embroider the design using 2 strands of the 6-strand embroidery floss throughout.
3. Work the lines in backstitch. The tiny little leaves are worked in detached chain stitch and the shading on the pumpkins is worked in straight stitch.
4. Stitch a seed bead where indicated by a small dot on the pattern, using a beading needle and a single strand of the lighter orange floss.

The entire pattern, shown 50% of actual size

Stitches Used in the Projects

This chapter is your guide to the stitches used in the projects. They are listed in alphabetical order for easy reference.

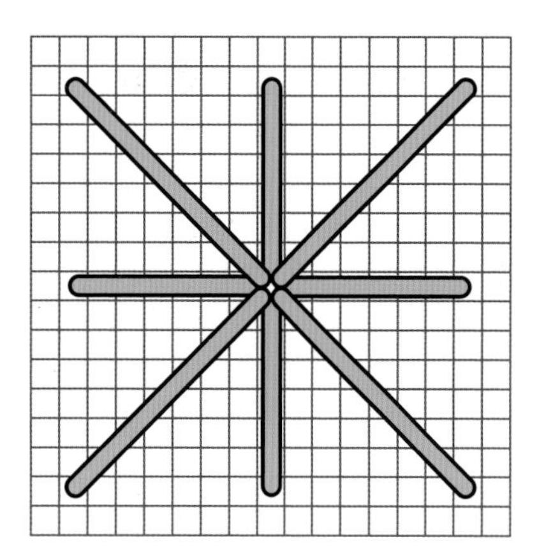

Algerian Eye

An Algerian eye can be used to make a small flower or a star, worked in rows and borders, stitched around the edges of shapes, or used as a scattered filling stitch. The rays of the stitch are worked from the outside towards the center, leaving a small hole, or eye, in the center. Any number of rays can be used, depending on the desired effect.

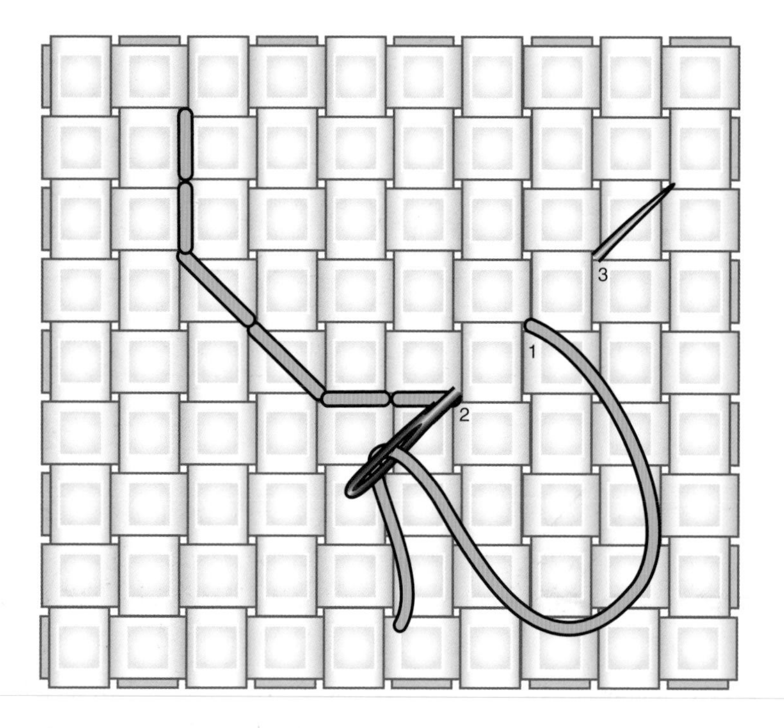

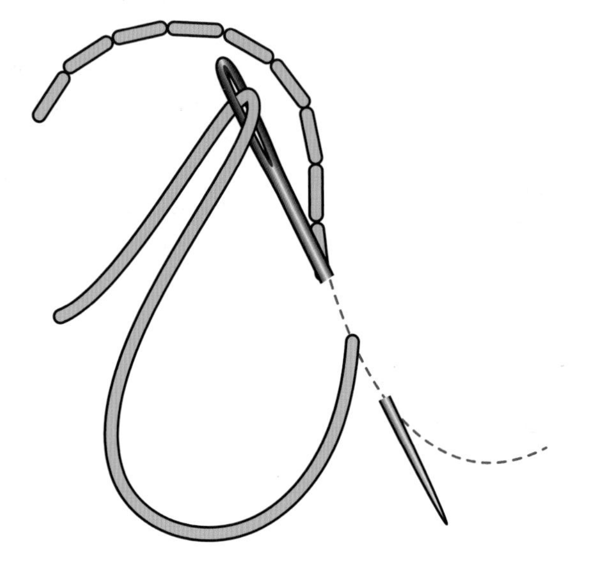

Backstitch

Backstitch is used to outline a shape and is worked in a motion of two steps forward and one step back. To work the stitch, bring the needle up through the fabric a stitch length's distance from the starting point and insert the needle at the starting point, working the stitch backwards. Bring the needle up again a stitch length's distance from the first stitch and continue working to the end. To work the stitch on Aida, work the stitches between the Aida squares, or diagonally across a square.

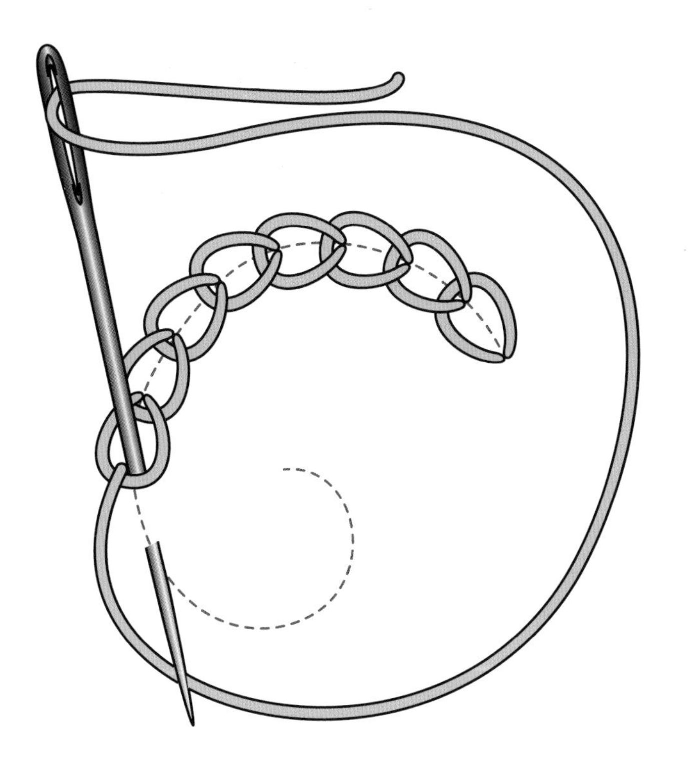

Chain Stitch

Chain stitch forms a thicker line of stitch with a decorative, chained effect. It can be used to outline shapes or as a filling by working closely spaced rows of stitching. The stitch is worked by forming a loop around the tip of the needle, with the needle insertion point in the same location as when you brought the needle up through the fabric. Each subsequent stitch starts inside of each previous stitch, forming a chain.

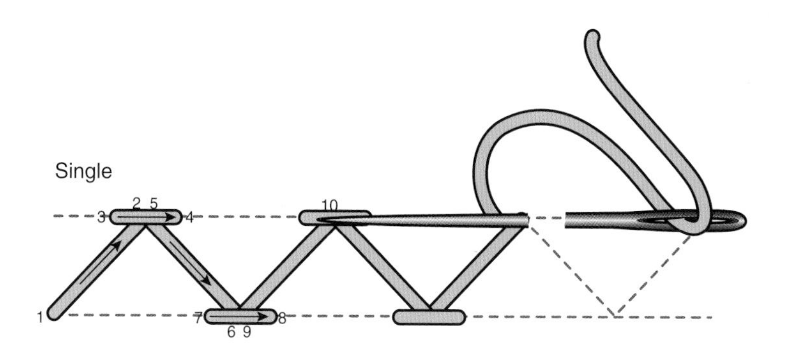

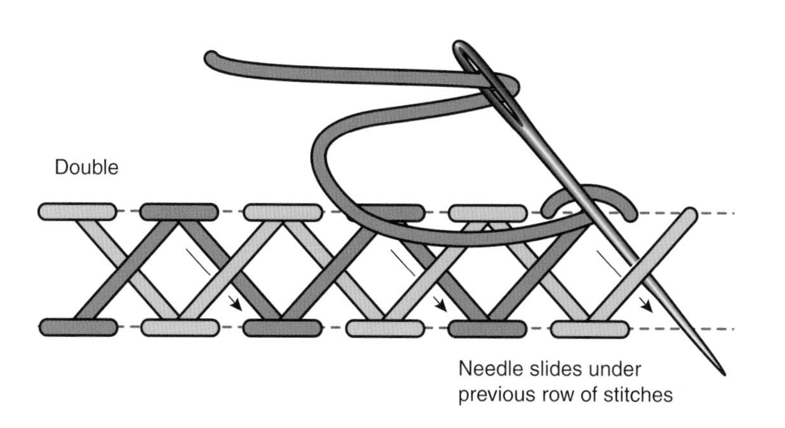

Chevron and Double Chevron Stitch

The chevron stitch is best used in rows and borders and features zigzagging stitch topped by a straight, horizontal stitch. It is easiest to work as a counted-thread stitch, but can also be used in surface embroidery by carefully marking the spacing on the fabric using a water-soluble fabric marker or pencil.

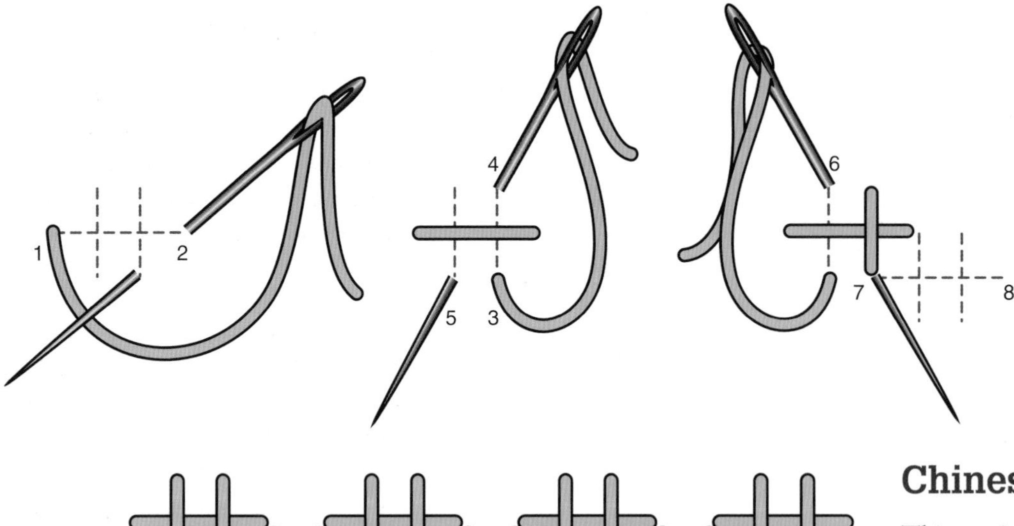

Chinese Cross-Stitch

This version of cross-stitch uses elongated stitches that cross horizontally over shorter vertical stitches. The stitches are staggered, with their corners meeting so that they form a band of stitching.

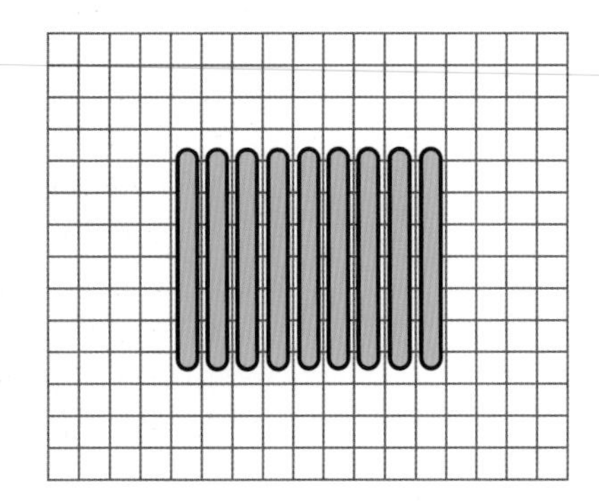

Counted Satin Stitch

Counted satin stitch is worked on evenweave fabric, with the stitches passing in between the fibers in the fabric. This stitch can be used to make individual motifs or geometric borders. It differs from regular satin stitch in that it is worked over a designated number of threads in the fabric to form a pattern, rather than following the outlines of a marked shape.

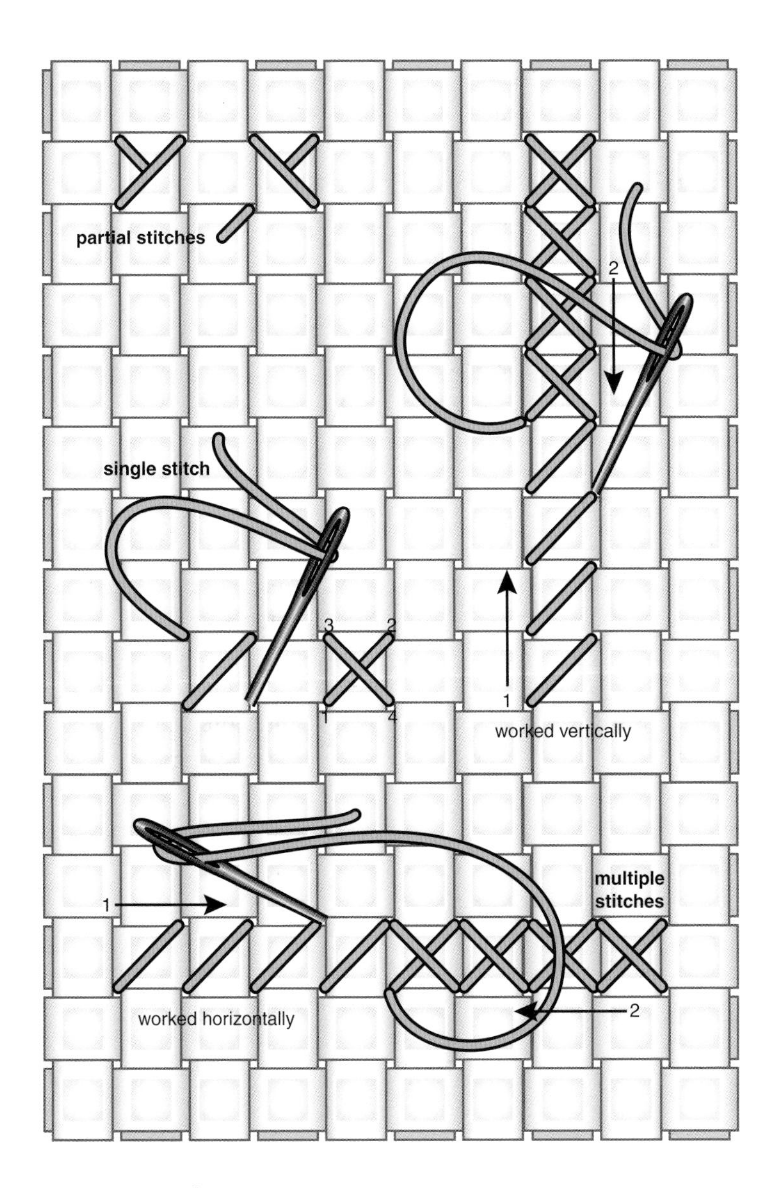

Cross-Stitch

Cross-stitch can be worked as a counted stitch over a single square on Aida fabric, or over two threads when using an evenweave fabric. It can also be used in a surface embroidery project by carefully marking the surface of the fabric. Each stitch is comprised of two diagonal stitches that cross in the center. They can be worked individually as well as in vertical and horizontal rows. Keep the stitches uniform by making sure the top stitch always crosses in the same direction, from upper left to lower right. When working a counted chart, you may also find that partial stitches are used, usually half or quarter stitches.

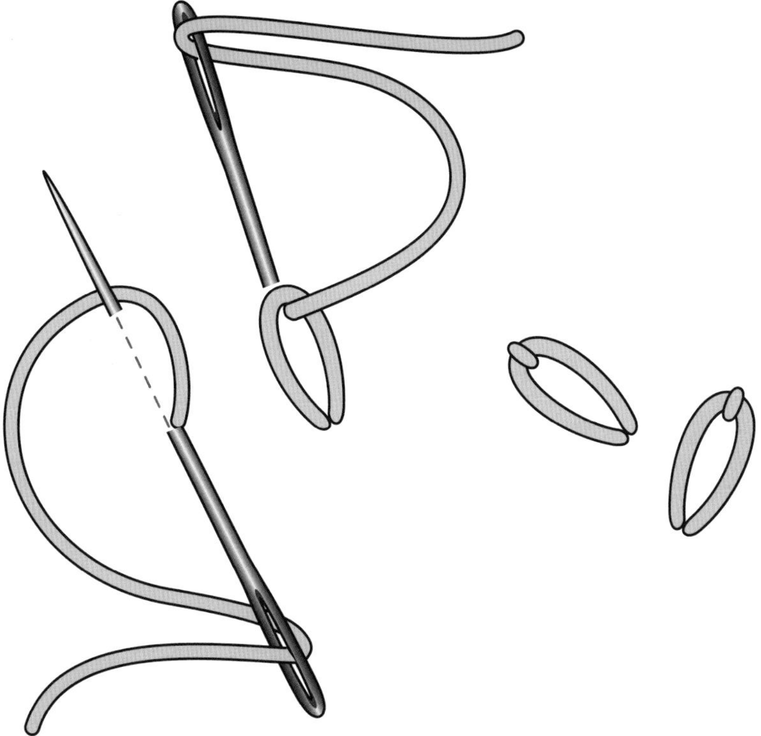

Detached Chain Stitch

Detached chain stitch is similar to chain stitch; however, instead of a chain of multiple stitches, a single looped stitch is made, held in place with a small tacking stitch at the opposite end of the loop. Detached chain forms the basis of the lazy daisy stitch (see page 82).

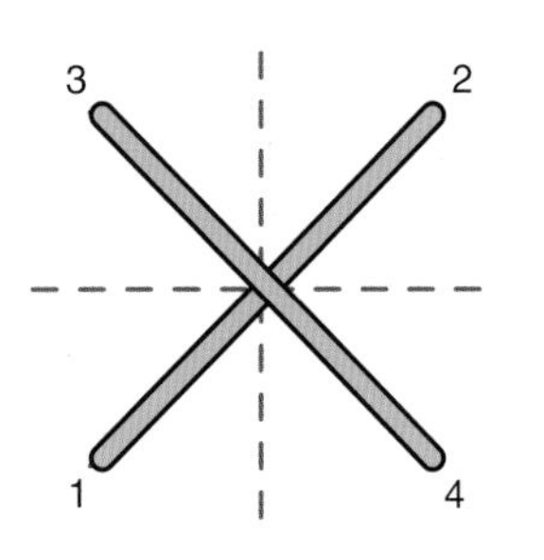

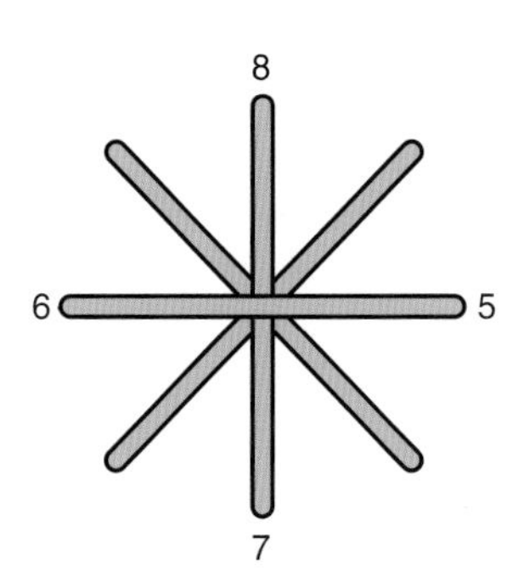

Double Cross-Stitch, or Star Stitch

A double cross-stitch is composed of a single, standard cross-stitch followed by an upright cross-stitch (see page 85). This stitch can be used to make stars, fillings, and decorative borders or bands in a project.

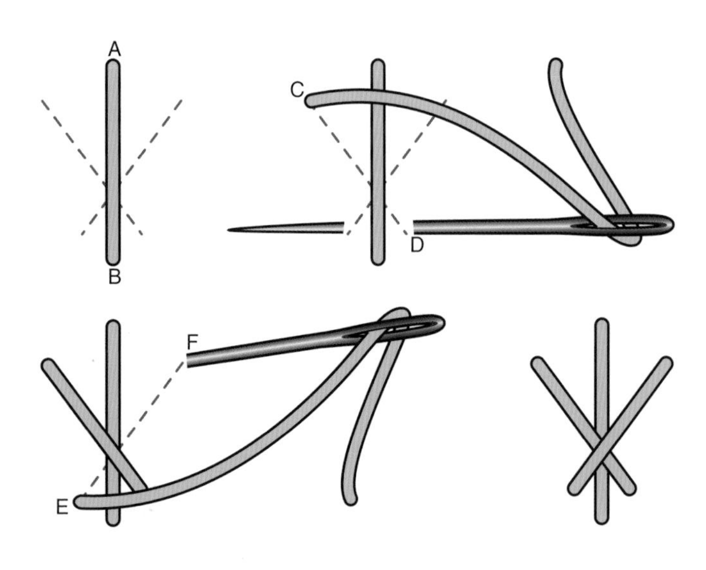

Ermine Stitch

The ermine stitch can be used individually, worked in rows, or used as a scattered filling stitch. It's made from a vertical straight stitch crossed by elongated diagonal stitches.

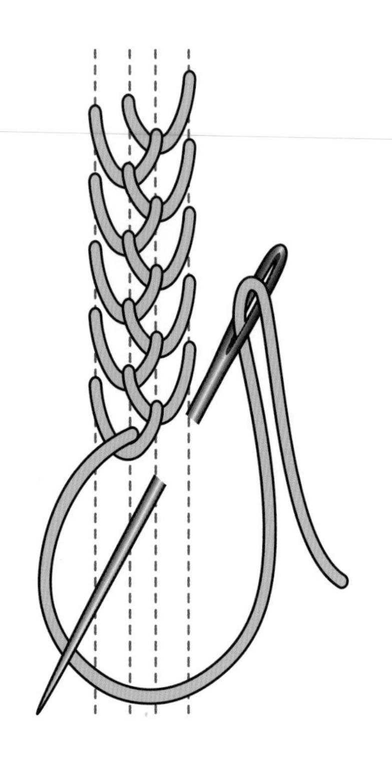

Feather Stitch

This versatile, textured stitch is the master of illusion. When worked closely spaced, the stitch makes a thick border or band. Worked father apart, the stitch is open, airy, and thin. Use this stitch in borders and rows or to outline shapes. It also mimics thorny stems and seaweed beautifully.

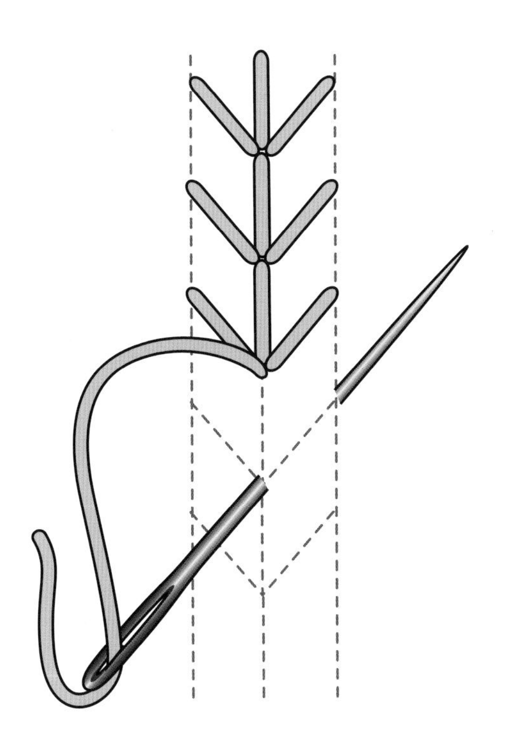

Fern Stitch

This easy, textured stitch is composed of sets of three straight stitches, with the insertion point for each stitch at the base of the three-stitch group. These groups are worked repeatedly along the line of stitching. Be sure to space and work each group uniformly for best results.

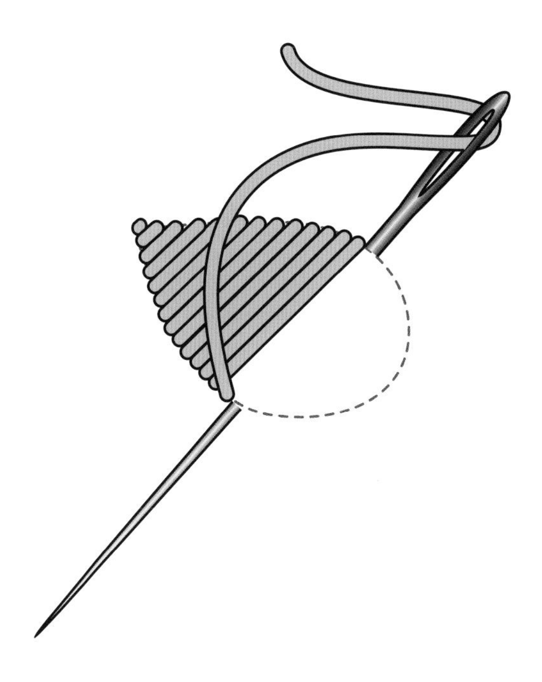

Flat Satin Stitch

Flat satin stitch is worked by laying down straight stitches without any padding or outlining.

Fly Stitch

The fly stitch can be worked along a straight or curved line and is heavily textured. The stitch is worked by making a horizontal stitch that is tacked in place with a small, vertical stitch worked slightly below it, forming a V shape.

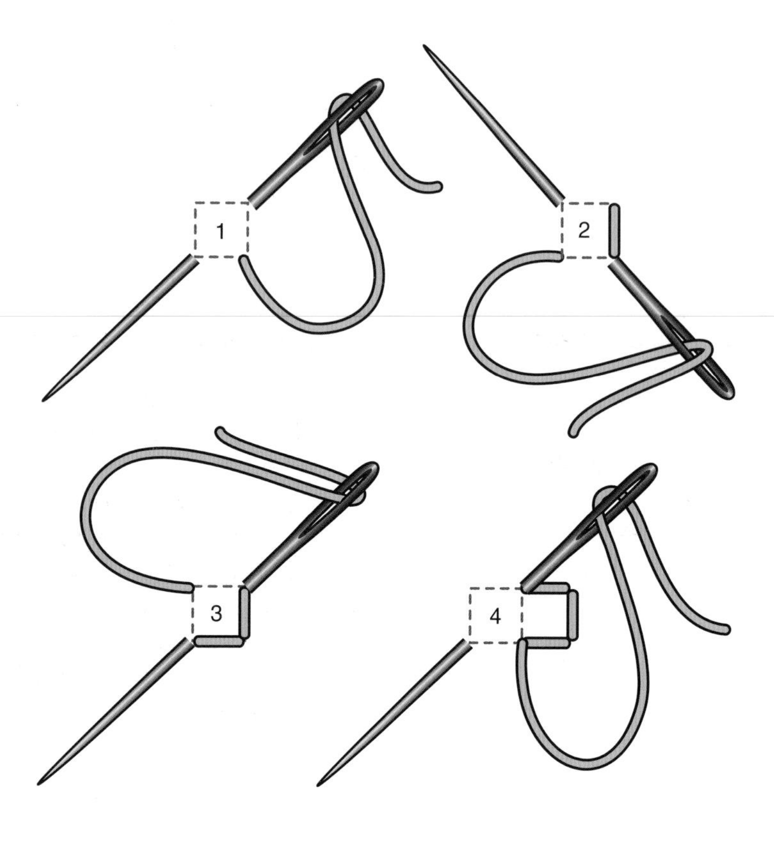

Four-Sided Stitch

This stitch is used to create small squares side by side, which can be used for borders and bands in a counted-thread project.

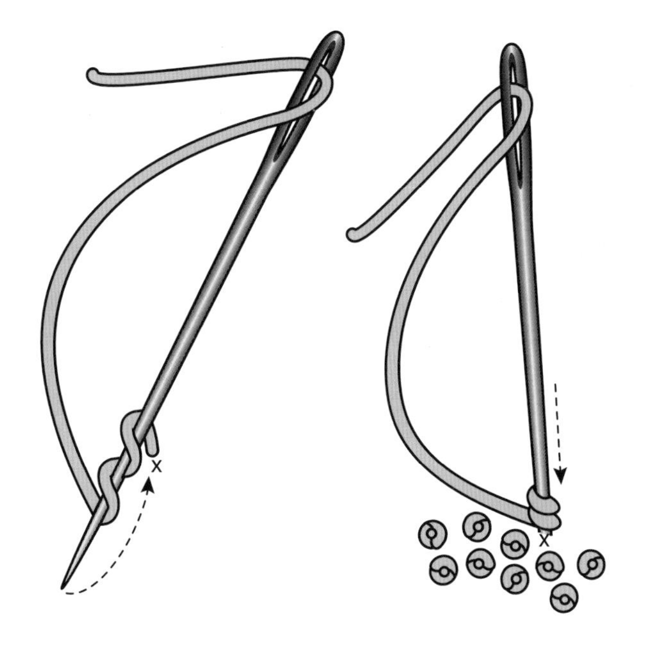

French Knot

French knots are easy to work once you've practiced them. To work a knot, bring the needle up through the fabric and wrap the working thread around the needle twice. Insert the needle back into the fabric very close to, but *not* in the same hole it just came out of, and pull the thread through, guiding it with your opposite hand as it passes through the fabric. Do not wrap too tightly or you'll have a difficult time pulling the needle through the knot. The thread should be against the needle, but not snug or tight. If your knot pulls through to the other side when working the stitch, try loosening the wrap a bit, and make sure you're not going down into the same hole. You'll need a bridge to hold the knot on the surface; usually just a fiber or two in the fabric will suffice.

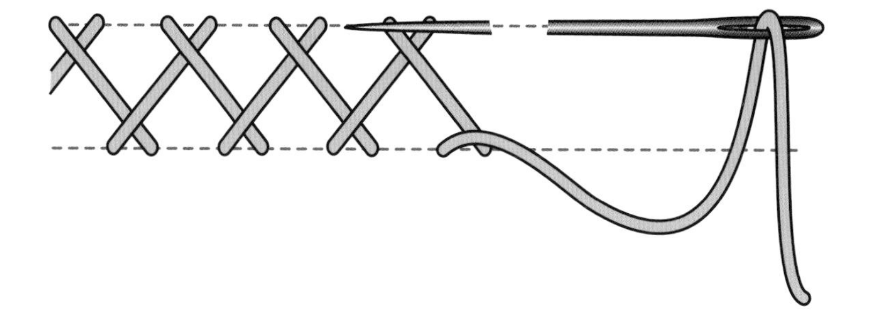

Herringbone Stitch

This decorative stitch forms overlapping zigzagging lines of stitching that are perfect for rows and borders or to outline a shape. It is easiest to work as a counted-thread stitch, but can also be worked in a surface-embroidery project by carefully spacing or premarking the stitches on the fabric. This stitch looks terrific with ribbon threaded through it.

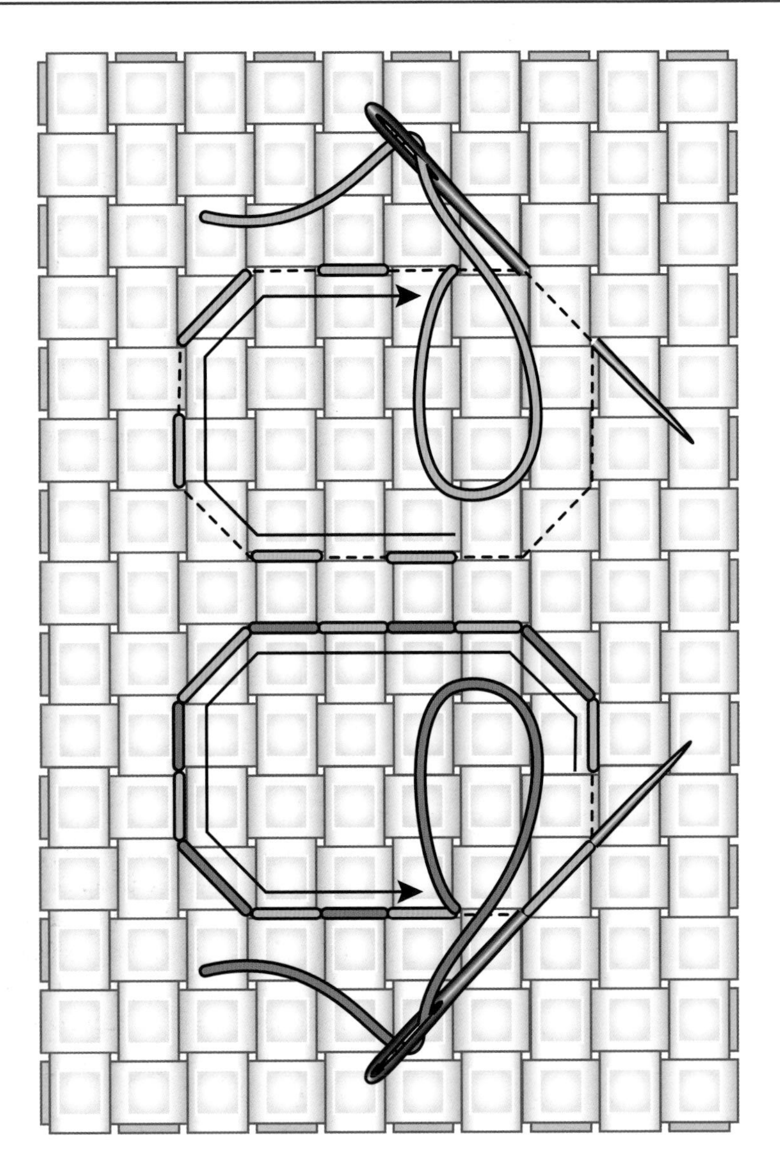

Holbein Stitch

The Holbein stitch looks similar to backstitch and is used to create a narrow line of stitching that looks the same on both sides of the fabric. Work the Holbein stitch in two passes.

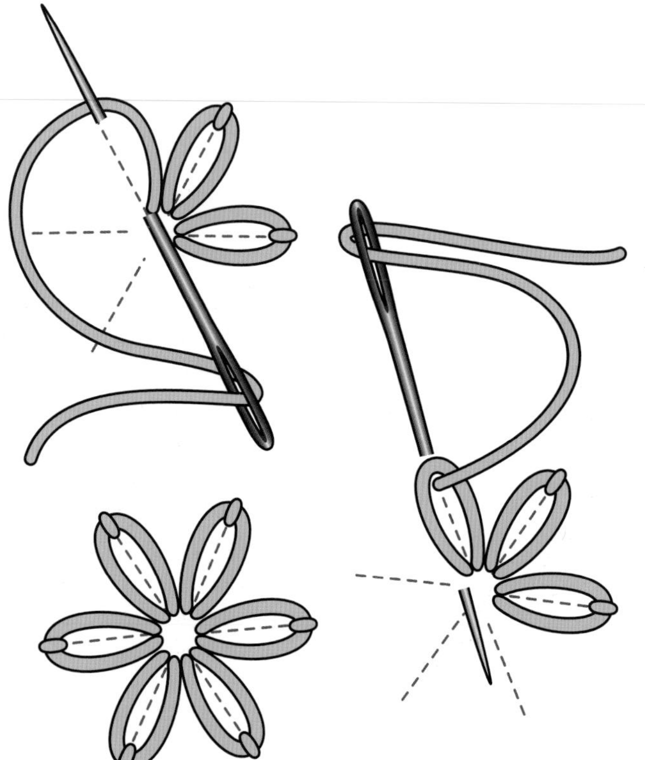

Lazy Daisy

A lazy daisy is a group of detached chain stitches (see page 77) worked around a center point to make a flower or small blossom.

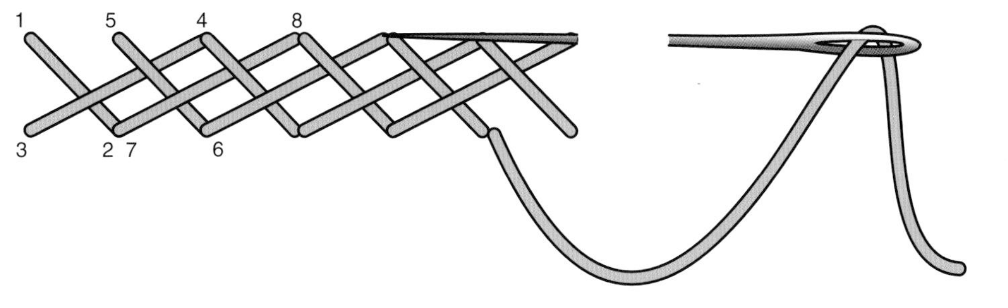

Long-Arm Cross-Stitch

The long-arm cross-stitch is used to make borders and rows. It can be worked as a counted stitch, or by carefully spacing the stitches in a surface-embroidery project. The first part of the stitch is worked the double width of a single cross-stitch, while the second part of the stitch is worked over a single width.

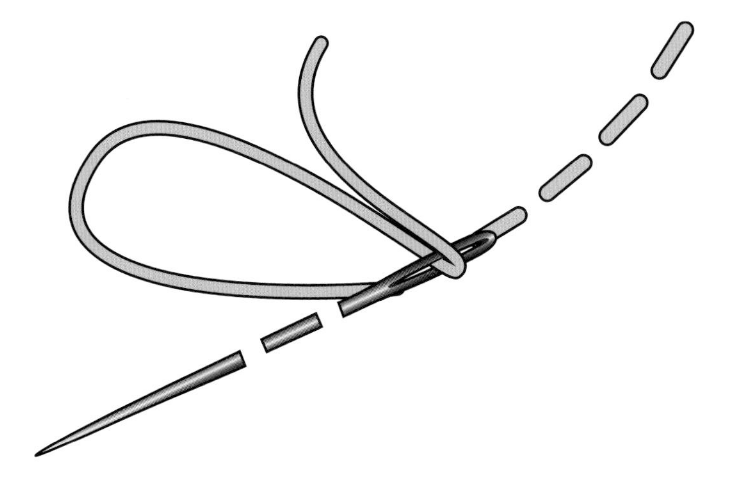

Running Stitch

Running stitch is worked using a basic, almost intuitive in-and-out motion of the needle. This stitch is typically used to outline a shape. It can be worked in any length and spacing, but should be kept consistent throughout the area being stitched.

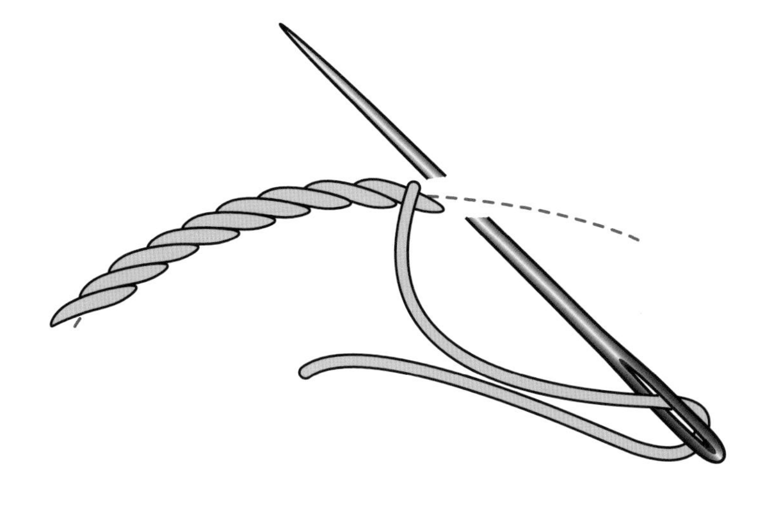

Stem Stitch

Stem stitch is a basic stitch that produces a solid line of stitching. This stitch can used to outline shapes or as stems and tendrils in a project. The stitch is worked by taking tiny stitches backwards along the outline of the shape. The working thread held below the needle, with each stitch slightly covering the previous stitch. Rows of closely spaced stem stitch can also be used as a filling stitch.

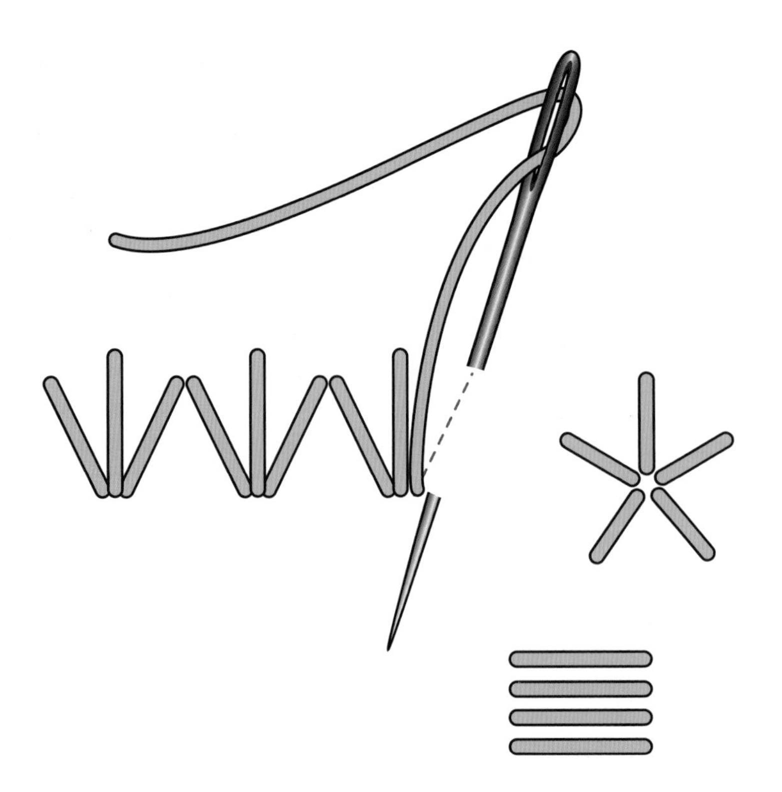

Straight Stitch

Straight stitch is just a single stitch, but can be used in different lengths and in groups to make other stitches or motifs. In the far-left example, three straight stitches have been used to make a decorative, repeating element in a border.

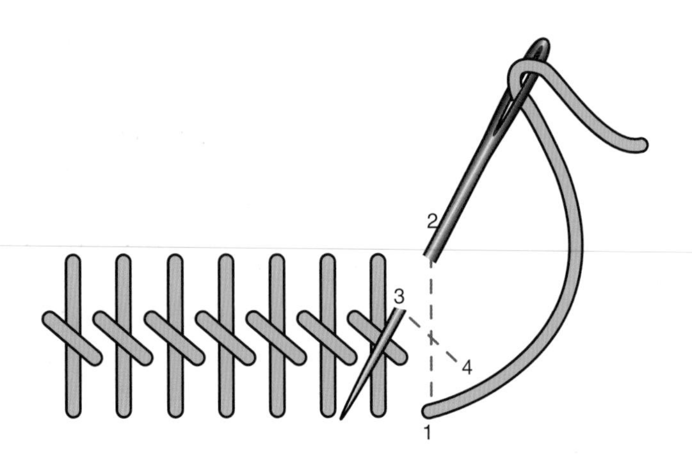

Tied Gobelin Stitch

This simple stitch can be used individually, in a row to make a border, or on multiple rows to make thicker borders. It's composed of two simple stitches: a single long upright straight stitch and a half cross-stitch that anchors the longer stitch to the fabric.

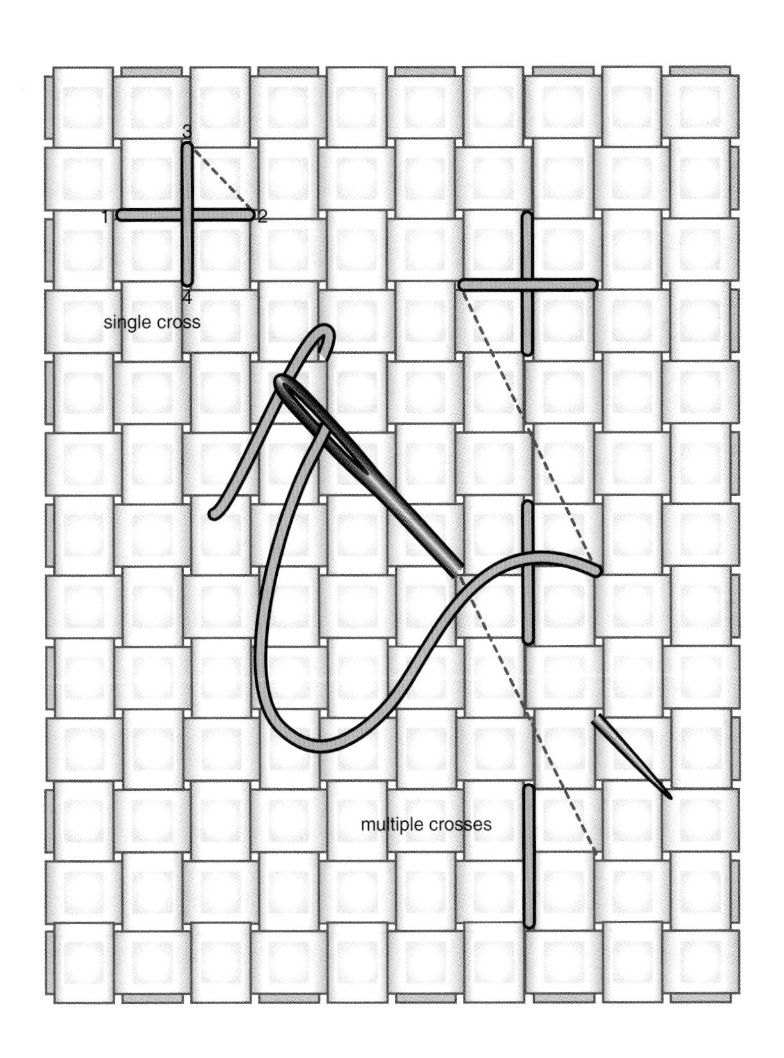

Upright Cross-Stitch

Upright cross-stitches are made up of a vertical straight stitch crossed by a horizontal straight stitch and can be used in surface embroidery or counted-thread projects. When worked on Aida fabric (shown here), the upright cross is worked over two intersections in the fabric.

Wheatear Stitch

The wheatear stitch can be worked as a textured border or band, in a straight line or along a curve. It is one horizontal stitch that has a detached chain stitch worked just below it, catching the stitch and making it curved.

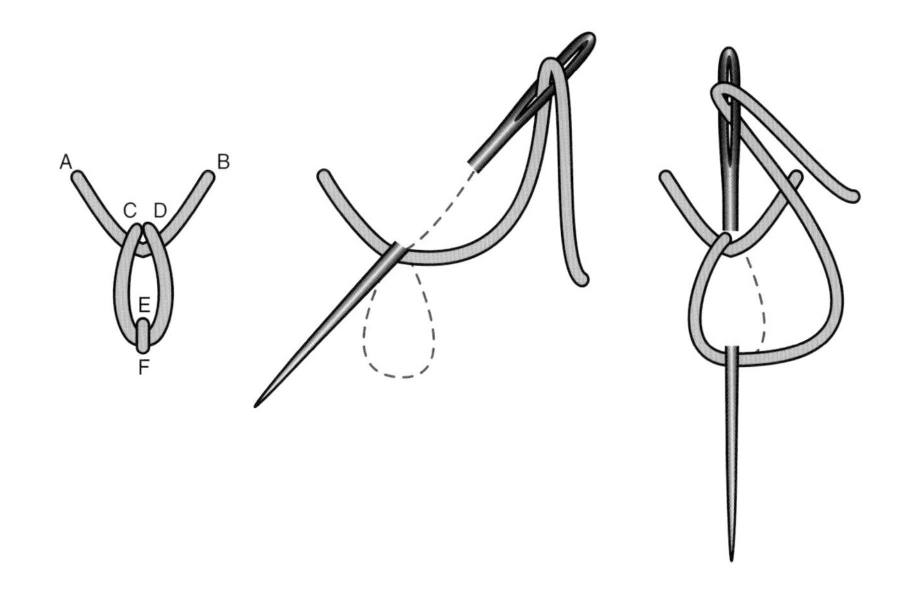

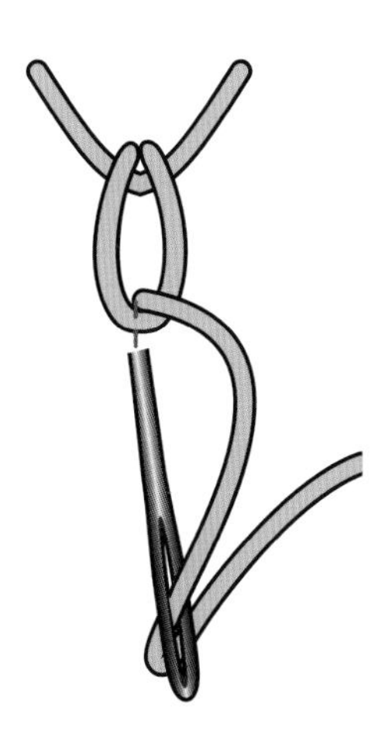

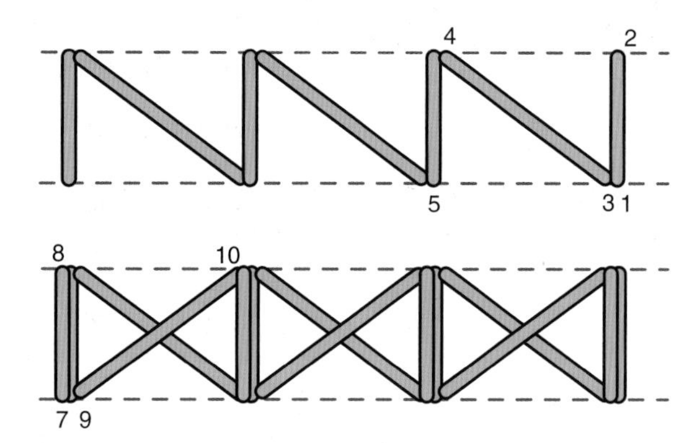

Zigzag Cross-Stitch

This band of stitching is made in two passes. The first pass is worked from right to left, in a pattern of an upright stitch followed by a diagonal stitch. The second pass is worked from left to right in the same manner. Work this stitch in a single band or border, or combine multiple rows for a wider band.

Finishing Touches

Here are some techniques for giving your sampler projects the perfect finish.

Mounting for Framing

1. To frame a finished sampler, cut a piece of acid-free foam-core board to fit the inside measurements of the frame you are using.
2. If desired, pad the board lightly by gluing a piece of flat (low-loft) cotton batting to it using acid-free glue.
3. Center the embroidered piece over the board and hold it in position using T-pins along the sides and corners to prevent shifting.
4. Fold the excess fabric to the back of the board and secure the piece using lacing stitches as shown. The stitching should be tight enough to hold the material in place, but should not stretch the fabric.
5. Remove the T-pins, insert the panel into the frame, and secure it in place.

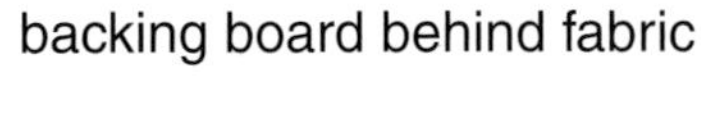

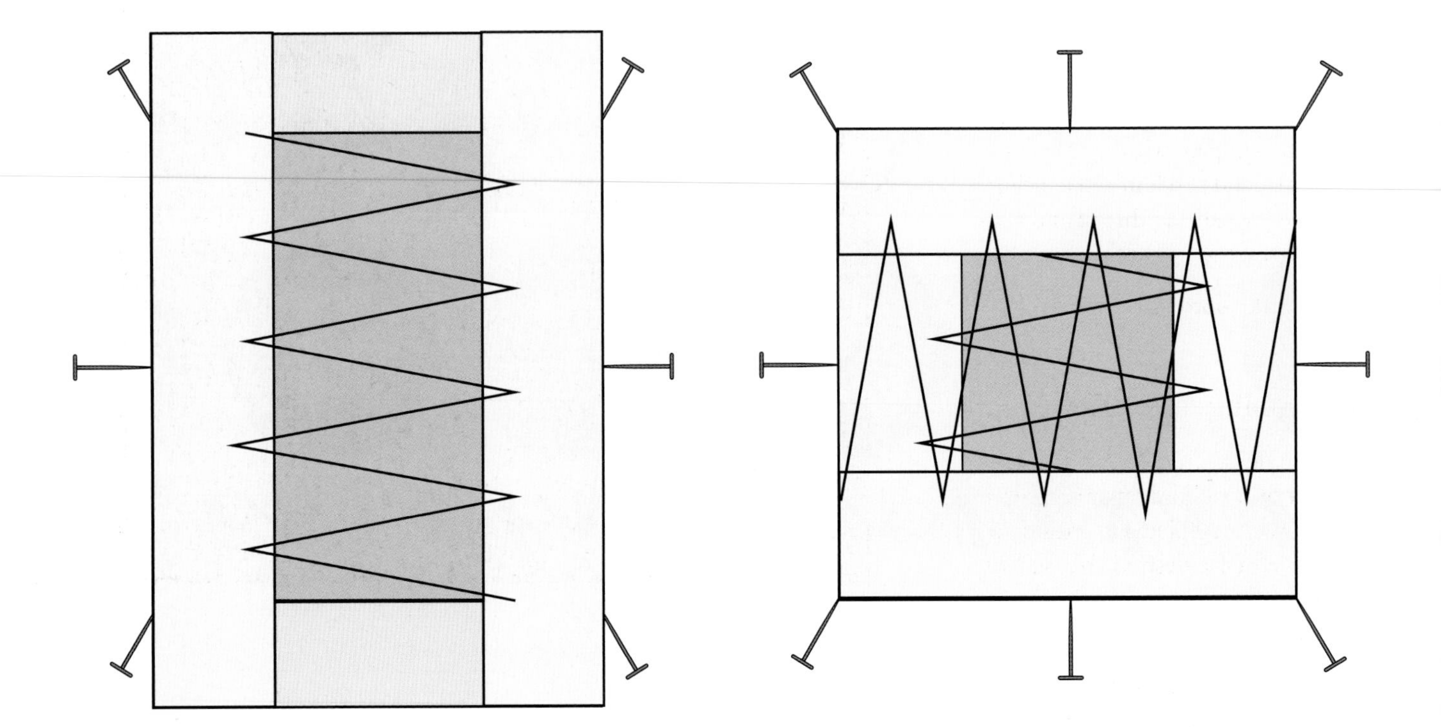

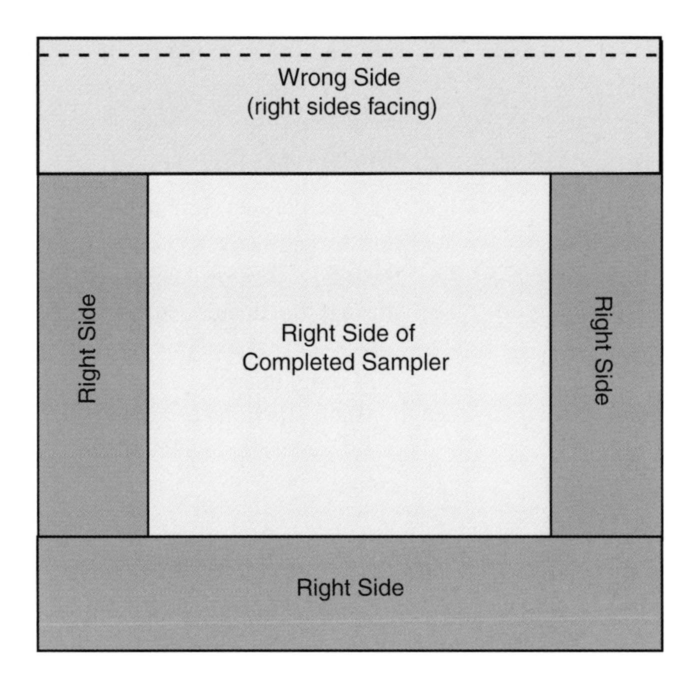

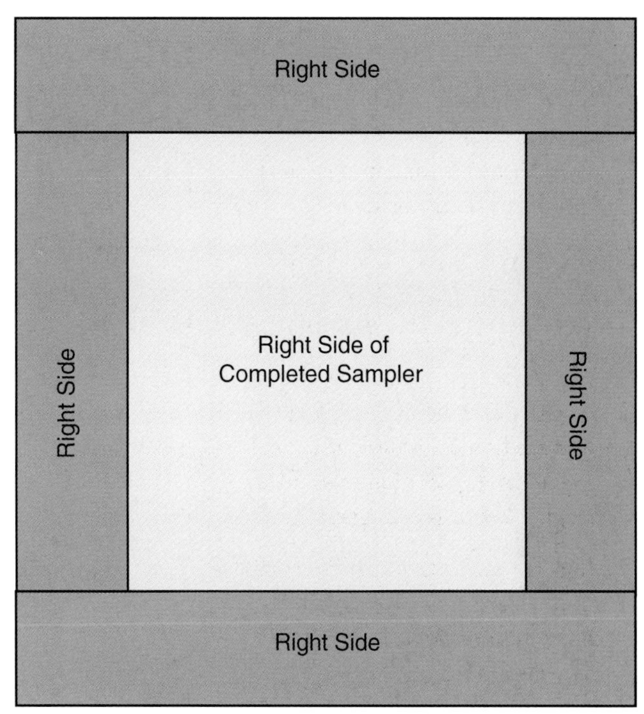

Making a Pillow Cover

Adding Borders to the Top

1. Trim the embroidered piece to within 1 inch of the desired size, so that you will have a ½-inch seam allowance on each side.
2. Cut the borders from the fabric.
3. Place the borders along the edges of the sampler, with right sides together, and stitch in place, using matching sewing thread and a ½-inch seam allowance.
4. Press the borders outwards and press.

Assembling the Pillow

1. Trim down the pillow top (either a piece with borders or a single embroidered piece) to within 1 inch of the desired size, so that you will have a ½-inch seam allowance on each side.
2. Cut a piece of backing fabric the same size as the pillow top.

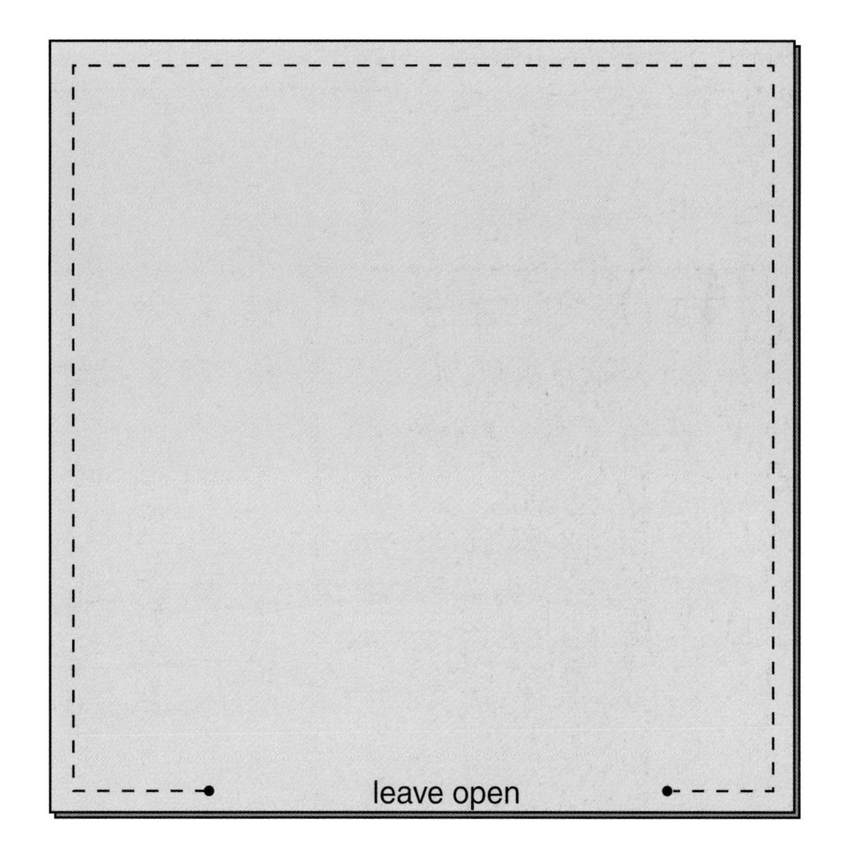

3. Place the top and back together with right sides together and stitch around, using a ½-inch seam allowance. Leave most of the bottom edge open.

4. Clip the corners close to—but not through—the stitching. Turn the pillow cover right-side-out through the opening at the bottom and insert a pillow form or stuff using fiberfill.

   Hand-stitch the bottom opening closed using matching sewing thread.

Making an Ornament

An ornament is made in the same manner as a pillow, but on a smaller scale. You can follow the same directions as for the pillow.

If the ornament is round, clip the outside edges after stitching to reduce bulk in the seam allowances.

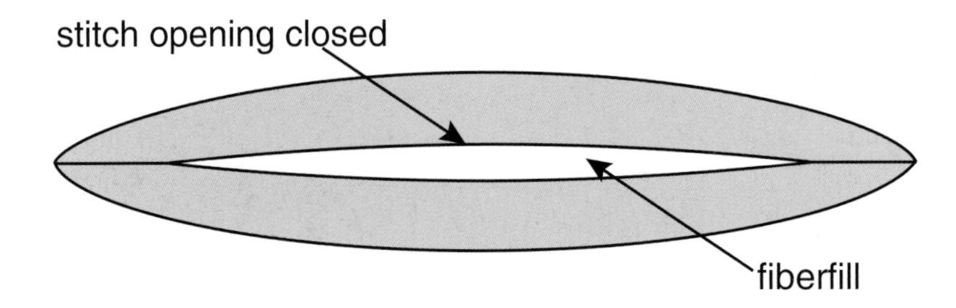

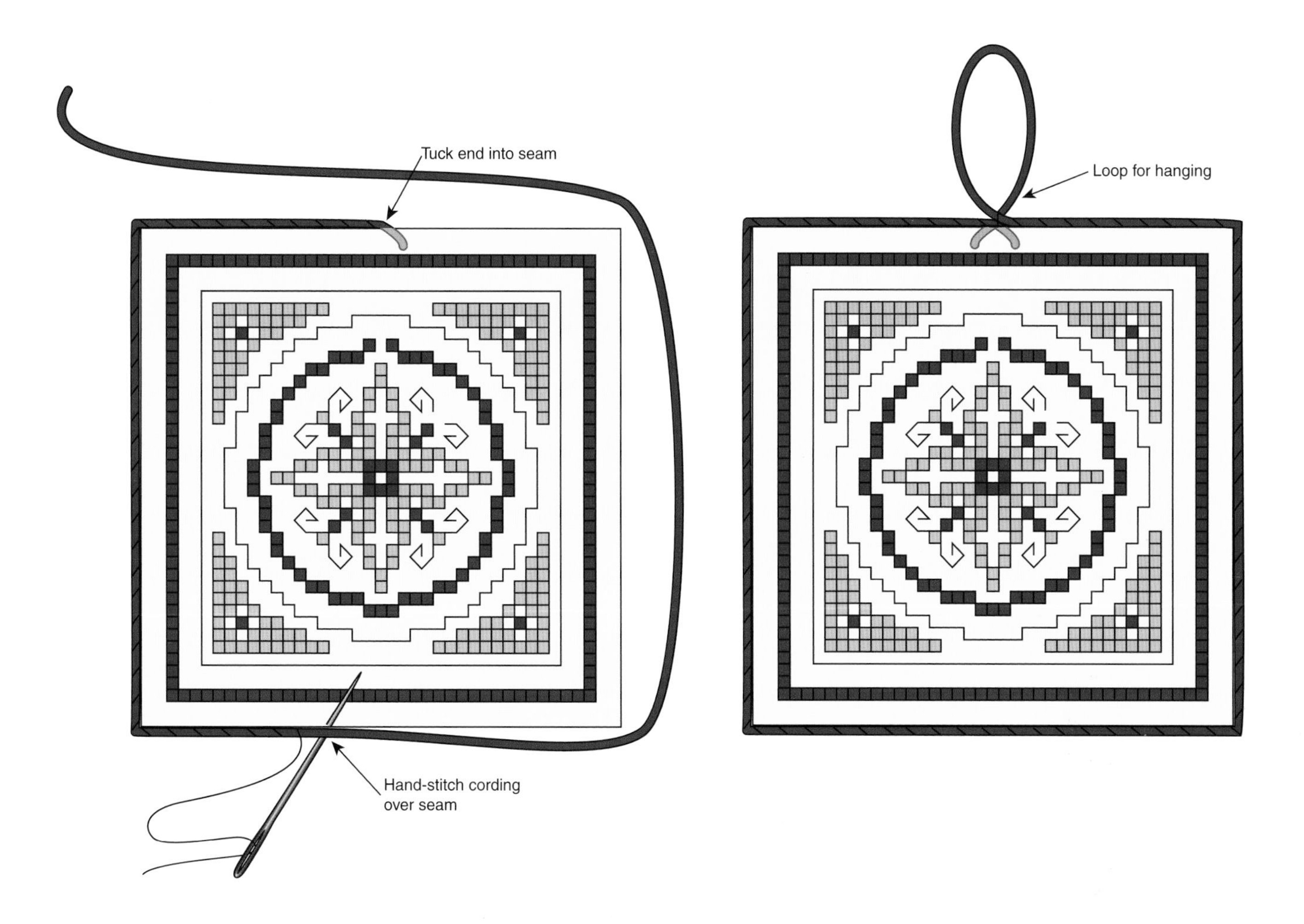

Attaching Cord Trim to an Ornament

1. Cut a length of trim about 8 inches longer than the circumference of the outside edge of the stuffed ornament.
2. Open a small hole in the seam at the top center of the ornament (just 1 or 2 slipped stitches should suffice) and insert ½ inch of an end of the trim into the hole.
3. Using sewing thread to match the trim, hand-stitch the trim around the outside edges of the ornament. The trim will cover seam line.
4. When you reach the starting point, cut away the excess trim, leaving a 5- to 7-inch tail.
5. Form a loop with the tail and insert ½ inch of the end into the same hole as the starting end.
6. Secure the ends in place with a few invisible stitches and close the hole.

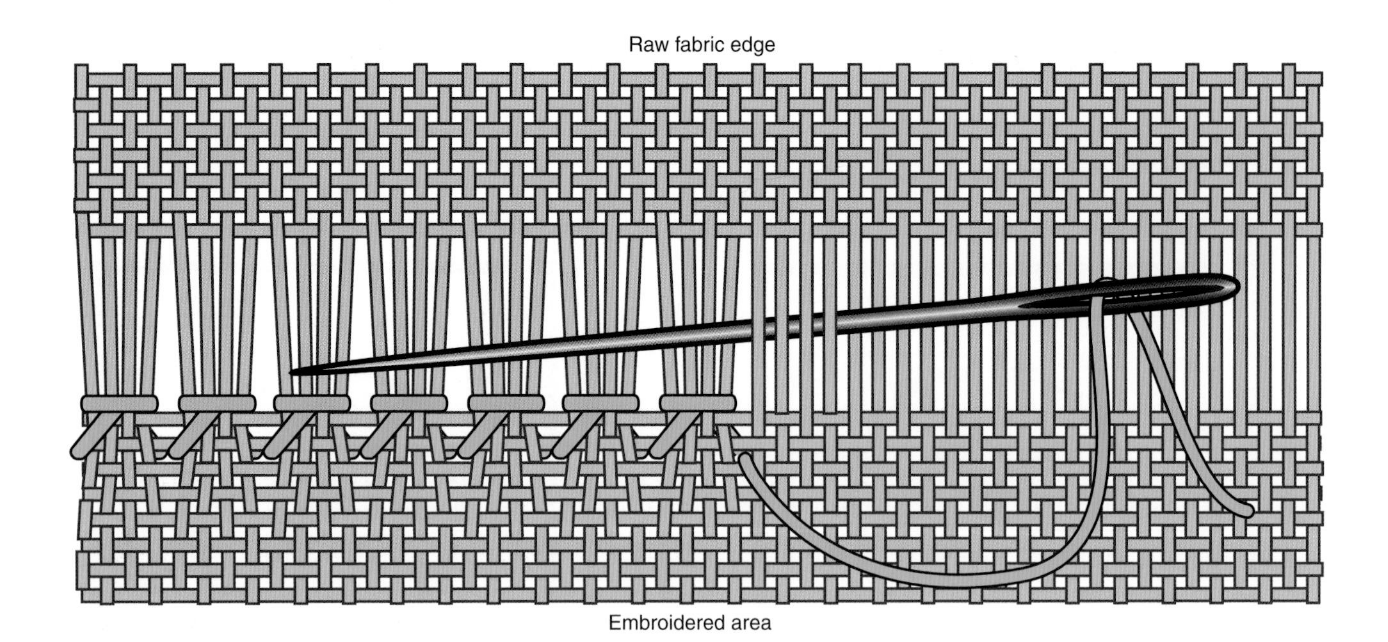

Fringing Fabric Edges

A fringed edge is a pretty way to finish small items like coasters or doilies and is actually very easy to do. This type of edge can be worked on nearly any evenweave fabric or Aida fabric.

1. Decide how far from the stitched edge you want the fringe to be. For example, if you want the fringe to start ½ inch from the edges, count the number of threads that are in the ½-inch space along all 4 sides.
2. Next, remove one or two threads just past the measurement in step 1, creating an open space. Do this along all 4 sides.
3. Work the basic hemstitch in the space going around 4 threads on an evenweave fabric or a block of threads on Aida fabric. The anchoring thread should be on the side embroidery side of the open space.
4. Determine how long you want the fringe to be and trim the fabric. For example, if the fringe will be ¾ inch wide, trim away the excess fabric around all 4 sides ¾ inch from the hemstitching.
5. Remove the fibers from the fabric along all sides to create the fringe.

Recommended Resources

Websites

Every stitcher has a favorite website featuring inspiration, tutorials, or supplies. These are a few of my favorites.

Cheryl Fall/NeedleKnowledge
http://needleknowledge.com

This site is a terrific resource for embroidery enthusiasts and features free patterns, stitch tutorials, links to educational videos, and other materials useful to stitchers.

DMC USA
http://www.dmc-usa.com

Free patterns and projects can be found in the separate stitching categories, but the mother lode of freebies is located in the DMC Club area. It's free—just sign up and sign in at http://www.dmc-usa.com/DMC-Club.aspx.

DMC's *Emma Broidery* Blog
http://dmc-threads.com

This blog, offered by DMC USA, features news and information about what's new on the needlework scene, as well as free patterns and projects for all stitching levels, and is updated several times per week.

Needle 'N Thread
http://www.needlenthread.com

This site run by Mary Corbet features an extensive collection of stitch videos, book and pattern reviews, tips and advice, free patterns, and resources for stitchers. Be sure to sign up for her free newsletter.

Royal School of Needlework
http://www.royal-needlework.org.uk

This UK-based group offers degree programs in the needlearts, including hand embroidery courses for all levels; conservation, restoration, and repair of antique embroideries; and an extensive collection of needlework.

Sharon B's PinTangle
http://pintangle.com

An excellent blog covering all things embroidery.

Guilds, Clubs, and Groups

The Embroiderers' Association of Canada (EAC)
http://www.eac.ca

This Canada-based nonprofit educational organization brings together people who enjoy needlework and wish to learn and share their knowledge. It offers classes and networking aimed at preserving and promoting traditional techniques.

The Embroiderers' Guild
http://www.embroiderersguild.com

This UK-based organization is known as an international voice for embroidery and offers members centralized and regional events, workshops, seminars, and exhibitions of fine historic and modern needlework. Its goal is to build awareness of stitch and textile art and offer inspiration to stitchers of all levels.

The Embroiderers' Guild of Queensland
http://www.embroiderersguildqld.org.au

This Australian guild's goal is to keep traditional forms of embroidery alive while also embracing new forms of stitching. It offers a wide range of classes for adults and children, which have been developed for skill levels from the beginner through to the accomplished embroiderer.

The Embroiderers' Guild of America (EGA)
https://www.egausa.org

Established in 1958, the EGA offers members the opportunity to learn a wide variety of techniques, as well as professional certification through online and correspondence courses and national seminars.

Guilds, Clubs, and Groups (continued)

The National Academy of Needlearts (NAN)
http://www.needleart.org

Established in 1985, NAN has devoted itself to the advancement of embroidery as an art form and provides education to those interested in furthering their embroidery skills as teachers, judges, artists, designers, authors, and technically proficient embroiderers.

The Stitchers' Village
http://www.stitchersvillage.com

This group is a global internet community, providing a unique place for the stitching community to gather, learn, discover, share ideas, and ask questions about embroidery and needlework.

Supplies for Embroidery

If you don't have a needlework retailer in your area, or you are unable to find needed items, here are several suggestions for online retailers. This list is by no means complete, but they are companies that I have used and trust.

ABC Stitch:
http://www.abcstitch.com

DMC USA Shopping:
http://www.shopdmc.com

Herrschner's:
http://www.herrschners.com

Nordic Needle:
http://www.nordicneedle.com

Yarn Tree:
http://yarntree.com/index.htm

Glossary

Aida. A sturdy cotton fabric used for cross-stitch that has an open weave with a mesh of squares. A single cross-stitch is worked over each mesh square.

Beading needles. Long, thin needles with small eyes that must be able to pass through the hole in a bead to attach it to the fabric.

Conversion chart. A chart that shows you the color numbers for the closest substitutes for threads produced by different manufacturers.

Counted-thread embroidery. The process of working a stitch over a designated number of warp and weft threads in the fabric, usually following a charted pattern. The pattern is not premarked on the surface.

Crocking. Dye transference resulting from washing or handling an embroidered piece.

Edge finishing. Securing the raw edges of fabric to avoid fraying as you work. Can include hemming, or overstitching with either a sewing machine set on zigzag stitch or a serger.

Embroidery. Decorative stitching in thread, floss, or yarn on a fabric ground.

Embroidery needles. Sharp needles with larger eyes. These are used when the needle must pierce the fabric rather than passing between the fibers in the fabric.

Embroidery scissors. Small scissors with sharp, pointed blades. The cutting blade is usually less than 2 inches long. The smaller size makes them easy to tote in a workbag when stitching on the go.

Evenweave. Fabric with an identical number of warp and weft threads per inch. The individual threads in the fabric are easy to count and are used in counted-thread embroidery.

Floss. A common embroidery yarn, featuring six individual strands of thread that are separated before using.

Hank. Embroidery thread purchased in a looped and twisted bundle. Hanks are not the same as pull-skeins, and thread must be unwound for use. Pulling thread from a hank will result in tangling.

Over-dyed floss. Floss that has been dyed with multiple colors that blend where the colors overlap.

Plainweave. Fabric with an identical number of warp and weft threads per inch. The individual threads in the fabric are tightly woven and difficult to count, making this a good fabric for surface-embroidery projects. May be made from cotton, linen, hemp, or other natural fibers.

Self-fringe. A method of securing the threads in an evenweave or Aida fabric with hemstitching, so that fibers in the fabric can be removed to make a fringe. The hemstitching holds the remaining fabric fibers in place and prevents fraying.

Skein. Embroidery thread in an easy-to-use bundle. The bundle is arranged so that the thread can be pulled from the skein to any desired length.

Stranded floss. Thread that is put up on a pull-skein in groups that can be separated, as in 6-strand embroidery floss.

Surface embroidery. Embroidery where the design is premarked on the surface of the fabric and worked in stitches that rest on top of the fabric.

Tapestry needles. Needles with elongated eyes and blunt tips. Used when the needle must pass between the fibers in the fabric rather than through them.

T-pins. Larger pins with a sharp point at one end and a folded, T-shaped end at the other. These pins are easy to grab and hold and are used to anchor fabric to completed projects to backings or blocking boards.

Thread count. The number of warp and weft threads per square inch of fabric. The higher the thread count, the tighter the weave.

Variegated floss. Floss that contains more than one shade of a particular color family, with evenly spaced color gradations.

Warp. Lengthwise threads in a plainweave or evenweave fabric.

Water-soluble. A product that can be dissolved in water or can be washed from the fabric.

Weft. Crosswise threads in a plainweave or evenweave fabric.

Color Conversion and Metric Equivalent Charts

Color Conversion Chart

DMC thread numbers and names have been used in the projects in this book. If these threads are not available in your area, use the chart below to select the same colors for other brands of thread. The colors may vary slightly between manufacturers; the table below shows the closest available match.

DMC Color	DMC	Anchor	Sullivans
Variegated Orange	51	1220	*
Variegated Red	115	1206	*
Very Dark Grape	154	873	45469
Dark Lavender	209	109	45041
Medium Lavender	210	108	45042
Medium Red	304	1006	45050
Black	310	403	45053
Very Dark Baby Blue	312	979	45056
Light Steel Gray	318	399	45059
Red	321	9046	45062
Rose	335	38	45068
Very Dark Salmon	347	1025	45072
Medium Coral	350	11	45074
Light Coral	352	9	45076
Dark Hazelnut Brown	420	374	45092
Light Brown	434	310	45095
Avocado Green	469	267	45104
Light Avocado Green	470	267	45105
Very Light Avocado Green	471	266	45104
Ultra Light Avocado Green	472	253	45107
Jade Green	505	210	45490
Dark Wedgewood	517	162	45114
Light Wedgewood	518	1039	45115
Very Light Ash Gray	535	401	45121
Medium Violet	552	99	45124
Violet	553	98	45125
Light Violet	554	96	45126
Cranberry	603	62	45138

DMC Color	DMC	Anchor	Sullivans
Very Dark Beaver Gray	645	273	45151
Bright Chartreuse	704	256	45164
Cream	712	926	45165
Dark Orange Spice	720	326	45167
Medium Orange Spice	721	925	45168
Medium Light Topaz	725	305	45170
Light Topaz	726	295	45171
Very Light Topaz	727	293	45172
Very Dark Olive Green	730	845	45174
Olive Green	732	281	45176
Medium Olive Green	733	280	45177
Light Olive Green	734	279	45178
Very Light Tan	738	361	45179
Tangerine	740	316	45181
Very Light Sky Blue	747	158	45188
Light Peach	754	1012	45189
Salmon	760	1022	45191
Medium Topaz	783	306	45201
Medium Delft Blue	799	136	45209
Very Dark Coral Red	817	13	45219
Baby Pink	818	23	45220
Very Light Golden Olive	834	874	45235
Dark Parrot Green	905	257	45254
Medium Parrot Green	906	256	45255
Light Parrot Green	907	255	45256
Medium Copper	920	1004	45266
Nile Green	954	203	45289
Pale Geranium	957	50	45292

DMC Color	DMC	Anchor	Sullivans
Light Pumpkin	970	316	45300
Deep Canary	972	298	45302
Dark Teal Green	3347	266	45344
Medium Teal Green	3348	264	45345
Baby Blue	3755	140	45378
Ultra Very Dark Emerald Green	3818	923	45415
Dark Straw	3820	306	45417
Straw	3821	305	45418
Hazelnut Brown	3828	373	45425
Terra Cotta	3830	5975	45427
Dark Bright Turquoise	3844	410	45442
Medium Bright Turquoise	3845	1089	45443
Very Dark Straw	3852	306	45450
Dark Autumn Gold	3853	1003	45451
Dark Rosewood	3857	936	45455
Dark Mocha Beige	3862	358	45460
Snow White	B5200	1	45002
Mediterranean Sea	4022	*	*
Monet's Garden	4030	*	35720
Princess Garden	4047	*	35722
Roaming Pastures	4050	*	*
Bonfire	4124	*	*
Desert Canyon	4126	*	*
Ocean Coral	4190	*	*
Wildfire	4200	*	*
Titanium	E317	*	*

*No actual match

Metric Equivalent Chart

1 inch = 2.54 centimeters
1 foot = 12 inches, 30.48 centimeters, or .30 meters
1 yard = 36 inches, 91.44 centimeters, or .91 meters

Acknowledgments

A hearty thank you goes out to my friends at DMC Threads in Kearny, New Jersey. They supplied the bulk of the materials used in this book.

I'd also like to thank my editor, Kyle Weaver, for asking me to write this book, and the entire Stackpole Books staff for their work on the book's publication. My grown daughters, Rebecca and Ashley, give me fresh, youthful ideas that always inspire me to push the limits with my designs and to "think young." My husband, Tony, never seems to mind the amount of time I spend each day stitching. To Mary Nevius, I'd like to express my gratitude for her years of friendship and her hard work on the NeedleKnowledge® website.

Visual Index

Welcome
to our Home

A
B
C
1
2
3
SCHOOL

Summer
Winter
Autumn
Spring

SMILE
AND BE
HAPPY